MANNERHEIM:
THE YEARS OF PREPARATION

MANNERHEIM:

THE YEARS OF PREPARATION

by

J. E. O. SCREEN

LONDON

C. HURST & COMPANY

Published in the United Kingdom by
C. Hurst & Co. (Publishers) Ltd.,
38 King Street, London WC2E 8JZ
Copyright by © J. E. O. Screen 1970, 1993
First edition 1970
2nd impression, corrected, and with new
preface and bibliographical material, 1993
3rd impression 2001
Printed in England
ISBN 0-90096-622-X

CONTENTS

LIST OF MAPS

PLATES

Between pages 54 and 55

Between pages 118 and 119

PREFACE

In an article entitled 'Marshal Mannerheim: the years of preparation', published in *The Slavonic and East European Review* in 1965, I attempted to outline Mannerheim's service in the Russian army and to suggest in what ways his experiences in Russia influenced his outlook and policy as a soldier and statesman in independent Finland. Although he described his years in Russia as preparation for his service in Finland, the preparation was as unconscious as his initial involvement in Finnish affairs was fortuitous. He followed a respectable Finnish tradition in joining the Russian army. He disapproved of russification measures in Finland, but continued to serve the Emperor loyally until the revolution destroyed his career in Russia and drove him to return to Finland as a refugee. The knowledge of Russia, its people and politics, which he acquired during thirty years' service in the imperial army, contributed to his sympathetic concern for the fate of that country and to his understanding of its strategic interests. Experience of the revolution accentuated his preference for a strong executive and sharpened his antagonism to what he regarded as the divisive and irresponsible influence of party politics. Finnish politicians of all parties could find something to dislike in his views and, except in times of national crisis, he remained cut off from political life.

Since I wrote this article, Professor Stig Jägerskiöld has published two important books, unfortunately not available in English, describing in detail the first part of Mannerheim's life. *Den unge Mannerheim* and *Gustaf Mannerheim, 1906–1917* add a great deal to our knowledge of his circumstances and opinions. As Marvin Rintala has written: 'Jägerskiöld's Mannerheim is far from the last word, but it is a major advance over the numerous Finnish versions in which the hero appears full-blown, at the age of fifty, in Helsinki in the winter of 1917–1918.' The least satisfactory aspect of Jägerskiöld's work, in my opinion, is his interpretation of Mannerheim's views on relations between Finland and Russia. In particular, his emphasis on the essential similarity between Mannerheim's political outlook and that of the Finnish 'constitutionalists' is open to question. I suggest in this book that Mannerheim's opinions were in several respects similar to those of the Finnish 'compliants': his views, like theirs, were based on recognition of the need for caution in the face of Russian power, and on loyalty to the common sovereign. Nor can it be over-emphasised that Mannerheim also felt a loyalty towards Russia. Because it will be some time before Jägerskiöld's work appears in English, and then only in an abridged form, I have described Mannerheim's formative years and service in Russia in considerable detail. In a chapter about his Asian expedition I point out that his reputation as an explorer is largely retrospective. Finally, I amplify the assessment in my original article of the importance of this period as the accidental background to the service in Finland on which Mannerheim's place in history depends. Mannerheim's treatment at the hands of historians and his biographers is the subject of an introductory historiographical essay.

Any writer on the early period of Mannerheim's life is bound to draw heavily on the detail in Jägerskiöld's work. I have, therefore, in general given page references only to actual quotations, and have followed the same principle with Mannerheim's *Memoirs* and the unpublished report he made to the Russian General Staff about his Asian expedition. A translation of this report was prepared for me by Cdr. Edgar P. Young, RN, retd. Dates are in New Style. Except in quotations, place-names in Finland are given in their Finnish forms. Russian transliteration follows the system used by *The Slavonic and East European Review*.

I am indebted to those who have talked to me about Mannerheim, especially Baroness Anastasie Mannerheim, Colonel O. R. Bäckman, Mrs. A-M. Borenius, and Father George Cheremeteff. Thanks to the very great kindness of S. de Witt, who wrote for me his reminiscences of the period when he was a second-lieutenant (cornet) and afterwards lieutenant and personal aide-de-camp to Mannerheim, I have had the benefit of an invaluable description of Mannerheim as a military leader during the First World War. I received from Professor Lauri Hyvämäki a long and helpful reply to a series of questions about Finnish politicial opinions. I have also received much kind assistance in Helsinki from Dr. Matti Klinge, from Professor Jarl Gallén and also from the staff at the University Library, the State Archives, the Military Archives, the Central Library for Military Research, the Finno-Ugrian Society, and the Foreign Ministry Archives. I am most grateful to my friends Catherine Raczyńska, Michael Branch and Jill Emery who read successive drafts of the manuscript and made useful and stimulating suggestions, and to Bob Hall who drew the maps. I also wish to thank Helen Piddington for typing the manuscript. Transcripts of Crown-copyright records in the Public Record Office appear by permission of the Controller of HM Stationery Office. Permission to quote from the report of Mannerheim's Asian Expedition was granted by the State Archives of Finland.

Acknowledgements are due to Cassell and Co. Ltd. and the Estate of the late Marshal Mannerheim for permission to quote from the *Memoirs of Marshal Mannerheim*; to the Hutchinson Publishing Group Ltd. for permission to quote from *Field-Marshal Mannerheim* by Tancred Borenius, *A Subaltern in Old Russia* by A. A. Ignatyev and *With the Russian Army 1914–1917* by Sir Alfred Knox; to Weidenfeld and Nicholson Ltd. for permission to quote from *Marshal Mannerheim and the Finns* by Oliver Warner; to Thames & Hudson Ltd. for permission to quote from *A History of Finland* by Eino Jutikkala; to Indiana University Press for permission to quote from *Finland in the Second World War* by C. L. Lundin; to the University of California Press for permission to quote from *Four Finns* by M. Rintala; to Stanford University Press for permission to quote from *Features and Figures of the Past* by V. I. Gurko; to Duke University Press for permission to quote from *The Russian Army under Nicholas I 1825–1855* by J. S. Curtiss; to Holger Schildts Förlagsaktiebolag, Helsinki, for permission to quote from *Sophie Mannerheim* by Berta Edelfelt and from *Den unge Mannerheim* and *Gustaf Mannerheim 1906–1917* by Stig Jägerskiöld; to Suomalais-Ugrilainen Seura (the Finno-Ugrian Society), Helsinki, for permission to quote from *Across Asia* by C. G. E. Mannerheim, *C. G. Mannerheim's Mapping Work* by A. K. Merisuo, *A Visit to the Saro and Shera Yögurs* by C. G. E. Mannerheim and *Suomen marsalkka Mannerheimin Aasia-teoksen valmistus-vaiheita* by K. Hilden; to the Otava Publishing Co., Helsinki, for permission to quote from *Mannerheim Suomen kohtaloissa* by Erik Heinrichs, *Gustaf Mannerheim* by Hannes Ignatius, *Lapsuuden muistoja* by Eva Sparre, and *Suuri rooli* by Yrjö Niiniluoto, and Suomen Historiallainen Seura (Finnish Historical Society), Helsinki, for permission to quote from *The Victors in World War I and Finland* by Juhani Paasivirta. The four photographs of Mannerheim are reproduced by courtesy of the Mannerheim Museum, Helsinki.

London J. E. O. SCREEN
November 1969

PREFACE TO THE SECOND IMPRESSION

In 1970, when the first edition of this book was published, it was possible to look forward to a clearer and more dispassionate assessment of Mannerheim's character and role in Finnish history because new sources were becoming available and old sensitivities in Finland were diminishing. That expectation has been amply fulfilled. Moreover, the collapse of the Soviet Union has removed a constraint on the expression in Finland of attitudes towards Russia and particularly towards the period of Soviet-Finnish conflict during the Second World War. Freed from the prospect of Soviet criticism, Finns can acknowledge historical truths and express their national feelings publicly. Naturally, these new conditions are prompting a reassessment of their wartime (and postwar) leadership, including Mannerheim. Evidence of the huge Finnish interest in Mannerheim can be seen in the unprecedented popularity of a major series of public lectures about him organised by the University of Helsinki in 1992, which resulted in the publication of *Mannerheim - sotilas ja ihminen* [Mannerheim - Soldier and Man] (Helsinki: Yliopistopaino, 1992).

Changes in Russia have also caused Russians to begin to see Mannerheim in a new light. No longer automatically condemned as anti-Soviet, he can be considered as sympathetic to Russia and his service in the imperial Russian army acknowledged as a positive formative experience. The positive nature of that experience for Mannerheim's activity in Finland is, of course, a theme of this book.

The assiduous work of historians and biographers has contributed greatly to a better understanding of Mannerheim's place in Finnish history and of his personality. However, relatively little new light has been shed on his years in Russia. An exception has resulted from the publication of Mannerheim's diary from the time of his service in the Russo-Japanese War, discovered in his now available personal papers (C. G. Mannerheim, *Päiväkirja Japanin sodasta 1904–1905* [Diary of the Japanese War, 1904–1905], Helsinki: Otava, 1982). With its criticism of Russian military inefficiency and its manifest professional outlook, the diary provides fresh evidence of Mannerheim as a keen combatant officer with an eye for the broad issues of leadership and the technical aspects of command. Publication of a fine selection of photographs Mannerheim took during his Asian expedition of 1906–08 (*C. G. Mannerheims fotografier från Asien resan 1906–1908. Photographs by C. G. Mannerheim from his Journey across Asia 1906–1908*, Helsingfors: Schildt, 1990) has formed part of a continued appreciative but realistic assessment of the non-military aspects of this reconnaissance mission.

Finnish historians have been re-evaluating the consequences of Finland's connection with Russia during the so-called autonomy period from 1809 to 1917. This connection formed the context of the service of Mannerheim and up to four thousand other Finns as officers in the Russian army and navy. The positive aspects for Finland of the autonomy period have been more clearly recognised and the dilemmas of those, like Mannerheim, who were serving in Russia when political relations between the Empire and Finland became strained can be regarded with greater sympathy. As Mannerheim understood at the time, Russo-Finnish relations could by no means be characterised in simple terms of black and white.

Thanks to the publication by Stig Jägerskiöld of a collection of Mannerheim's private letters (C. G. Mannerheim, *Brev från sju årtionden* [Letters from Seven Decades], Helsingfors: Söderström, 1984) - half of which date from before 1918 - the warm nature of Mannerheim's relationship with his family and friends can be discerned from his own words. Jägerskiöld's biography of Mannerheim was completed in eight volumes and the author also wrote a single-volume version which has been translated into English (*Mannerheim, Marshal of Finland*, London: Hurst, 1986). The scale of Jägerskiöld's work and his extensive sources - including much diplomatic material - command respect. Although President J. K. Paasikivi's diaries were not then available, in writing of the period after 1941 Jägerskiöld used to good effect the diaries of the German General Waldemar Erfurth and those of Mannerheim's friend, the Finnish diplomat Georg Achates Gripenberg. Jägerskiöld presents an admiring and imposing portrayal of Mannerheim, although its credibility is reduced by his obvious reluctance to recognise that Mannerheim's actions were influenced by his nature as a human being, possessed of prejudices and sometimes fallible.

Writing on the Finnish Civil War of 1918 has emphasised the difficulties that arose for Mannerheim as commander of the White Army because he was an outsider, an alien figure in a Finnish context, a view exemplified by Anthony F. Upton in his study of *The Finnish Revolution, 1917–1918* (Minneapolis: University of Minnesota Press, 1980). These difficulties contributed to Mannerheim's years in the political wilderness between 1919 and 1931 - a period that has recently attracted attention. Martti Ahti has shown in his book, *Salaliiton ääriviivat* [Outlines of a Conspiracy] (Espoo: Weilin & Göös, 1987), that the activist conspirators who wanted to seize power in Finland in the summer of 1919 so that Finland could attack the Bolsheviks in Petrograd hoped to involve Mannerheim as leader of their *coup*. Mannerheim was also considered by some of the leaders of the right-wing Lapua Movement of 1930 as a possible dictator of Finland but no links between them and Mannerheim have been found. The *coup d'état* was not part of Mannerheim's thinking or his style.

He was, on the other hand, capable of the occasional bold stroke. His decision to disarm the Russian garrisons in Ostrobothnia in January 1918 was one example: it began a victorious campaign. Another, which led to defeat and near-disaster, was his decision in February 1941 to rely on German support to resist Soviet pressure on Finland and to take part in the German attack on the Soviet Union, which he had correctly deduced was going to take place. The definitive study by Mauno Jokipii of the background to Finland's participation in renewed war with the Soviet Union in 1941, *Jatkosodan synty* [The Origin of the Continuation War] (Helsinki: Otava, 1987), has confirmed Mannerheim's crucial involvement in the realignment of Finnish policy at that time, reinforced by the threat of resignation as commander-in-chief if he did not get his way.

Resignation or the threat of it was a weapon which Mannerheim used not infrequently. His resignation in May 1918 as commander-in-chief was unexpectedly to create for him the possibility of return to office as regent when Germany's defeat necessitated the abandonment of the Finnish government's pro-German policy. He twice used the threat of resignation in 1939 when chairman of the Defence Council and he considered - somewhat unjustifiably - that defence needs were being neglected. His role as chairman of the Defence Council has been examined and clarified by Kari Selén in his *C. G. E. Mannerheim ja hänen puolustusneuvostonsa 1931-1939* [C. G. E. Mannerheim and his Defence Council, 1931-1939] (Helsinki: Otava, 1980). Mannerheim's achievements during that period were not inconsiderable in terms of the organisation of Finland's defence establishment and even over appropriations. He strove hard but ultimately unsuccessfully for military co-operation with Sweden, a subject considered by Martti Turtola's book, *Tornionjoelta Rajajoelle* [From the River Tornion-joki to the River Rajajoki] (Porvoo: WSOY, 1984).

Much of relevance has been published on Finland in the Second World

War, on politics, foreign policy and military operations. The biography by Martti Turtola of General Heinrichs, Mannerheim's chief of staff for much of that time, *Erik Heinrichs - Mannerheimin ja Paasikiven kenraali* [Erik Heinrichs - Mannerheim's and Paasikivi's General] (Helsinki: Otava, 1989), has revealed differences between the two men over the conduct of the war although their personal relations remained good and Heinrichs played an important part in the writing of Mannerheim's memoirs. Paradoxically, revelation of the true collaborative nature of Mannerheim's memoirs has been accompanied by greater critical attention to them as a historical source.

Mannerheim has recently been considered more 'in the round', as a person as well as a soldier and statesman. The biography by the writer Veijo Meri, *C. G. Mannerheim, Suomen marsalkka* [C. G. Mannerheim, Marshal of Finland] (Porvoo: WSOY, 1988) has played a significant part in this. Elegantly written and drawing on expert advice, Meri's biography captures Mannerheim's complex character and shows how his humanity survived popular adulation and the isolation of great responsibility. Meri's portrait is reinforced by the detail of Mannerheim's private life provided in Sakari Virkkunen's *Mannerheimin kääntöpuoli* [The Other Side of Mannerheim] (Helsinki: Otava, 1992).

However, in the final analysis Mannerheim owes his place in history to his achievements as a Finnish soldier and statesman. Those achievements - and failures - must be the subject of continual reappraisal: such is the lot of great men, and Mannerheim is no exception for he is part of the fabric of Finland. Perhaps, as Laura Kolbe has written, the 1990s could become the period of 'the Russian Mannerheim', while Finland's increasing internationalisation may open the way to sympathetic recognition of his un-Finnish character as a European gentleman. (Laura Kolbe, 'Marski - ihminen', in *Mannerheim - sotilas ja ihminen*, p. 106.) Undoubtedly, Mannerheim's hopes for a trustful relationship with a reformed Russia must find an echo in present day Finland. His 'years of preparation' still command attention.

In addition to this new preface, a short supplement of works on Mannerheim has been appended to the bibliography. Otherwise, apart from a few typographical corrections, the text of the 1970 edition remains unchanged.

London   J. E. O. SCREEN
March 1993

INTRODUCTION:

THE 'UNKNOWN' MANNERHEIM
OF HISTORY

Few men have been so passionately admired and violently hated as
Gustaf Mannerheim. His role as commander-in-chief of the victorious
White army in the Finnish civil war of 1918 made him a controversial
figure. The Whites interpreted their triumph over the Finnish socialists
and Russian Bolsheviks as a 'War of Liberation', a fight against internal
and external enemies which constituted the last act of the long struggle
of the Finnish people to preserve its national existence and win its freedom
from oppression.[1] Mannerheim became admired, even idolised, as a
symbol of victory, in spite of the reservations some Finnish Whites felt
about his former service in the Russian army, his antipathy to Germany,
and advocacy of intervention in Russia. The defeated Finnish socialists
long hated him as an oppressor, recalling with bitterness the 'White
Terror' that followed the civil war and in particular the deaths of thousands of Red Guards in prison camps, for which they held him responsible.

Not surprisingly, comment about him by Marxist writers has been
persistently hostile. A Swedish communist wrote a pamphlet entitled
' "Mannerheim the bloody" or "the white devil" '.[2] Suppression of the
revolution in Finland and support of intervention in Russia prompted
savage attacks on him in the Soviet press.[3] He was often referred to as
'the butcher' or 'the slaughterer', and Soviet leaflets dropped on Finland
during the Winter War depicted a blood-stained 'Executioner Mannerheim'.[4] Preparations in Finland for the commemoration of the centenary
of his birth were criticised in the Red army newspaper *Krasnaya zvezda*
as an attempt by reactionaries to revive the anti-Soviet policy he had led.[5]

The events of 1918 emphasised a division in the Finnish nation which,
in general, caused Mannerheim to be seen against a background of
political and historical prejudice that precluded an impartial appraisal of
his actions and character. Both sides – and different groups on each side –
sought to write the history of the war to their own advantage. Immediately

I

after the war Mannerheim set up a committee to collect documents and write a factual account of the course of events:[6] his real aim was to ensure the history of the war was written 'as we ourselves have wanted it'.[7] The outcome of this initiative, *Suomen vapaussota vuonna 1918*,[8] gave Mannerheim's version of events; the other major collective work on the war, *Suomen vapaussota*,[9] was the version of the activists and *Jägers*. The important history of the war by Colonel J. O. Hannula,[10] which appeared somewhat later, concluded that the result of the War of Liberation had been to free the country and erect a dam against Bolshevik barbarity. This was typical of the tone of much other literature of the period.

The official view of the war as a War of Liberation, not a civil war or class war, played its part in giving Mannerheim a national rather than a 'White' image. He contributed to the spread of this conception by his withdrawal from politics after his defeat in the presidential election of 1919 and by his attempts to be conciliatory towards the vanquished. He did, however, remain a focus for right wing sentiment, and like the right wing became increasingly disturbed by the political course taken by the republic. He welcomed the Lapua movement which arose in 1929–30 with the aim of extinguishing communism in Finland. The pressure exerted by this movement had the indirect result of his recall to an official position in 1931 as chairman of the Defence Council. After returning to office, Mannerheim began to play a more positive conciliatory role. At a parade in 1933 commemorating the war he stated that there was no need to ask where anyone had been fifteen years previously, or in other words, on which side they had fought in the civil war. Between 1933 and 1939 his image became increasingly national and less partisan until, the outbreak of the Winter War, Finland united under his military leadership. Mannerheim's prestige, position and authority as commander-in-chief and eventually as president during the war period made him important as a symbol of national unity and independence and afforded greater justification for the traditional right wing conception of him as a patriot and a hero. In these circumstances, the already remote possibility that he might be written about objectively disappeared.

The first biography of Mannerheim, by his military and political collaborator and friend, Major-General Hannes Ignatius, was published in 1918.[11] It took the form of a brief biographical introduction, followed by a collection of Mannerheim's speeches and writings. Ignatius indicated and justified Mannerheim's attitude to various controversial issues: he wanted Finland to acquire East Karelia but not in such a way as to rupture relations with a future Russia; others had decided not to march on Petrograd as he had wished; his attitude to the Åland islands question showed how Finnish he was – he put Finland before everything. All this had obvious propaganda value, as did the reprinting of some of his speeches. Illumination of his character was incidental, for example when Ignatius revealed that Mannerheim was finally persuaded not to resign over the issue of German intervention in the war by an appeal not to ruin the greatest task of his life. A larger collection of the speeches of 'Finland's liberator and regent', together with some adulatory material about him, had appeared in 1919.[12] Ignatius wrote the biographical article on Mannerheim in the popular reference book *Oma maa*[13] but no major biography appeared during the 1920s. Mannerheim's emergence from retirement was followed by a resumption of writing about him and he was the subject of a considerable number of books published during the Second World War and the years immediately preceding it. For the most part, they characterised him as a great military leader and statesman, an explorer and a humanitarian. These themes were first outlined in the important biography, *Sotamarsalkka vapaaherra Mannerheim*, by Kai Donner, published in 1934.[14]

Donner was a scholar, though not a historian. However, as Juhani Paasivirta has observed, his work revealed the difficulty of a biographer who had too great an admiration for his subject and did not, in general, write critically, even if he made some attempt to consider political problems objectively.[15] The starting point of his book about 'the White General . . . who led our fight for liberation'[16] was the article he had written about Mannerheim for the biographical reference work *Kansallinen elämäkerrasto*.[17] He aimed to set out Mannerheim's views by quoting extensively from his speeches. The closeness of his relations with Mannerheim – he wrote with his consent and received his assistance –[18] compelled him to be delicate: for example, he did not mention the expulsion from the Corps of Cadets, and although he referred to the loyalty Mannerheim had felt towards Russia before the revolution he did not develop this theme. He explained that Mannerheim had preserved his Finnish patriotism while in Russia, and that service there had enabled him to develop a far-sighted political outlook. This explanation of the value of his service in Russia and of the history of his patriotic opinions became generally accepted. Donner conveyed Mannerheim's bitterness in 1919 and his gratification at the new spirit of the 1930s, and in particular the pleasure he received from his promotion to Field-Marshal. There was considerable emphasis in the book on his capacity, leadership and achievements as a statesman and a description of his humanitarian work, but little about his personality.

An advantage of Donner's association with Mannerheim was the permission he received to quote from the as yet unpublished diary of his Asian expedition. Later writers were to go further than Donner in depicting Mannerheim as an explorer and his expedition as a scientific achievement rather than a military reconnaissance. The publication in English in 1940 of Mannerheim's Asian diary, and of a volume of articles by various scholars about his scientific work, fostered his image as an explorer and provided new material on this aspect of his life for subsequent writers.[19] The diary also appeared in Swedish, Finnish, Danish and Dutch.[20] The first biographer to describe and assess Mannerheim's expedition in proper perspective as a military task was Stig Jägerskiöld in 1965.[21]

Mannerheim's seventieth birthday in 1937 assumed the character of a national festival. A *Festschrift* in his honour, *C. G. Mannerheim*, was published the same year.[22] It began by tabulating his ancestors and describing the history and achievements of his family. His sister, Eva Sparre, contributed some recollections of his childhood. Other articles eulogised him as a statesman and as a soldier and commander to whom 'Finland could always have recourse again for aid in a moment of need'.[23] A former ADC attempted to characterise him 'as a private individual and as a person'. Kaarlo Hildén, who had been entrusted with the task of editing for publication the diary of the Asian expedition, wrote of him as an explorer and man of science. His work as chairman of the Finnish Red Cross and as founder of General Mannerheim's Child Welfare Association was not forgotten. There was even a description of his home. The pattern and reverential tone of this *Festschrift* were to be repeated several times, notable on the occasion of his seventy-fifth birthday and soon after his death.[24]

The Winter War aroused throughout Europe considerable interest in the Finnish commander-in-chief. The biography by Donner was translated into Danish in 1940[25] and Norwegian in 1941.[26] New works were published during 1940 in France,[27] Hungary,[28] and Great Britain.[29] Tancred Borenius, a Finn who was Professor of the History of Art at University College, London, wrote his *Field-Marshal Mannerheim* 'to supply the want of a book in English in which the Field-Marshal would be envisaged from the double point of view of the interest of his personality as such, and of his relation to Finland's past and present'.[30] This book, which drew on Donner's work and the *Festschrift* of 1937 as well as the author's personal acquaintance with Mannerheim, was a clear expression of the 'white' interpretation of Finnish history and a flattering account of Mannerheim's achievements. The biography by Paul Rodzyanko was even more laudatory. Its author, an emigré Russian officer, did not share the same background as Mannerheim's Finnish biographers and therefore showed less understanding of Finnish history but greater interest in Mannerheim's service in Russia. The value of Rodzyanko's work was that his contacts with those who had known Mannerheim before the revolution, and his own acquaintance with him as a junior officer, enabled him to produce a description of Mannerheim's character, life in Russia and reputation in the imperial army which, though heavily overdrawn, had an underlying credibility. Borenius had mentioned Mannerheim's inability to suffer fools gladly, and his biting sarcasm, but had not attempted a balanced appraisal of his character. Rodzyanko, too, was inhibited in this respect by his regard for Mannerheim. However, in mentioning that he was 'a very frank admirer of feminine beauty'[31] and that he scorned money, Rodzyanko touched on topics difficult to mention in Finland while Mannerheim, who resented any intrusion into his private life,[32] was still alive.

In 1937 J. O. Hannula had written about Mannerheim as commander-in-chief during the War of Liberation.[33] This was not intended to be a full biography but included some information – mainly from Donner's book – about Mannerheim's life before and after 1918. An enlarged edition was published in 1942. The other biography by a Finn available during the Continuation War (1941–44), *Suomen sotamarsalkka* by Anni Voipio, a journalist, was revised and reprinted for the last time in 1953.[34] The author's aim was to bring the Marshal closer to the general reader and to reveal 'the life work of the greatest Finn of our time', the proper assessment of which remained the task of the historian.[35] An American historian described the book as 'worshipful'.[36] In this respect it did not differ from other works on Mannerheim published during the same period.

Mannerheim retired from the presidency in 1946 and had completed his memoirs before he died on 28 January, 1951; they were published in 1951 and 1952,[37] and abridged and translated into several languages.[38] In the main, the chapters of the memoirs were drafted by his staff, who based them on conversations with him as well as on documents. Mannerheim corrected and rewrote these drafts with such attention to factual and stylistic detail that the final version of the memoirs undoubtedly bore the character of his own work. Almost devoid of personal material, the memoirs constituted the last act of his life, his testament to the Finnish people and to Finland's friends abroad, providing a consistent, if one-sided, account of Finnish history, and a vindication of his actions. He tried to show that although Finland had made mistakes, the policy of the great powers had made its fate in the Second World War inevitable. He concluded with a lesson on the value of national unity and a statement of faith in the ability of the nation to survive. Even in the memoirs he remained the symbol of Finnish independence.[39] The value of his account of events was recognised though its scale was too broad to fulfil the hopes and needs of researchers.[40] The accuracy of that account did not go unchallenged; for example, Onni Talas, a member of Svinhufvud's government in 1918, criticised various points Mannerheim made about the civil war and its aftermath.[41] John I. Kolehmainen wrote that 'the account reveals not only an occasional lapse of memory, but a disposition to rewrite the record to the marshal's advantage.'[42] The publication of other memoirs and studies, particularly on the Second World War period, made it possible to indicate and rectify Mannerheim's lapses and prevarications. An American, C. Leonard Lundin, commented: 'Whether his statesmanlike qualities . . . were as marked as the casual reader of his memoirs or biographies would gather remains open to dispute. And the question: Was he always a truthful man? is one to which the critical reader, comparing his book with the others we have looked at, would hesitate to return an unqualified 'Yes'.'[43]

In assessing Mannerheim's memoirs and the work of other Finns published after the armistice of 1944 it must be remembered how difficult it was – and indeed still is – for Finns to write objectively about the recent war. Finland had been defeated and forced to acknowledge responsibility for the war. It had become plain that the country's continued independence was conditional on the retention of the goodwill of the Soviet Union. The former line of foreign policy had been repudiated. The questions were bound to arise whether pre-war policy had been wrong, whether war could have been avoided, whether peace could have been made sooner. Professor Arvi Korhonen described some of the questions asked about recent Finnish history and the reasons for them in the introductory chapter of his important book *The Barbarossa Plan and Finland*.[44] The re-examination of the 1930s and 1940s was a painful process. One writer left it to posterity to judge whether the Continuation War had been a mistake or not.[45] It was easy to perceive Mannerheim's importance as a living guarantee that Finland's fate during the war would not be destruction, and to acknowledge the epoch-making significance of his decisive part in leading Finland to a hard peace in 1944 and in taking the responsibility for its consequences.[46] However, his responsibility for involving Finland in the Continuation War was largely passed over. A British historian, A. F. Upton, has described that responsibility and indicated the terrible consequences for Finland of Mannerheim's error of judgment in believing in 1941 that Germany would defeat the Soviet Union. His book, *Finland in Crisis*,[47] was heavily criticised, particularly for his argument that policy decisions were made by an inner ring consisting of Mannerheim, Ryti, Walden, Witting and Rangell, men who were unresponsive to public opinion, beyond the control of parliament and who acted at times unconstitutionally.[48]

Despite the difficulties, a more realistic assessment of Mannerheim has developed gradually since his death. There was a final flowering of the type of tribute familiar from earlier years when in 1953 the Finnish nobility published a *Festschrift* in honour of 'its greatest member of all time'.[49] However, even that work contained an article on Mannerheim as a commander-in-chief by General Erik Heinrichs – his chief of staff for much of the Continuation War – which suggested shortcomings in his method of command.[50] Heinrichs considered that although Mannerheim was remembered in Finland as the Finn who led the nation's defence, he was also a European *grand seigneur* with the mentality of a crusader in his attitude to Bolshevism in 1918 and 1919. Heinrichs believed Mannerheim's approach to life was that of a warrior, fighting enemies in peace as well as war, extracting all he could out of every situation and out of what life offered. A few years later he developed his ideas about Mannerheim in a two-volume biography[51] which has a special value because of his personal relationship to his subject and detailed knowledge of many of the events about which he wrote, although he undoubtedly knew more than he revealed.

In his first volume, *The White General*, Heinrichs recognised that Mannerheim was used by Finland in periods of danger and laid aside when more peaceful times came. He said very little about his service in Russia but aptly remarked that he returned to Finland in 1917 'almost like a stranger from a sunken world'.[52] He asserted that Mannerheim's ability to perceive political factors, to use people and situations to further his aim, and his strength of will – and in 1918 his faith in victory – made him a leader unique in Finnish history. He analysed the reasons for

B

Mannerheim's resignation in 1918 and emphasised his differences with the government over policy towards Russia and his fundamental belief that the allies would win the war. Heinrichs expressed the conflict Mannerheim experienced between his duty towards Finland and his desire to be the liberator of Russia as well. He behaved delicately towards Russia but would not compromise over Finland's independence nor permit encroachments on its sovereignty. He conducted a tireless fight in Paris against the representatives of Sweden and Russia, the two cultures closest to him after that of Finland. He overcame the temptation of the scheme suggested by a group of Finnish activists in the summer of 1919 to use his power as regent to dissolve parliament and intervene in Russia – a triumph of his sense of duty over his crusading spirit. This was an unusually clear statement of Mannerheim's regard for Russia and its practical consequences.

In his second volume, *The Marshal of Finland*, Heinrichs stated that, unlike a hero of modern times, Mannerheim had not risen from the masses, and the goals he admired were far above those of everyday life. Although his personality was often described as unapproachable, those who had served close to him remembered him not as an elegant lord but as a great man whose strength of will they admired. Heinrichs, naturally, shared this admiration. He was prepared to criticise Mannerheim, for example over the unfairness of the comments in his memoirs about the Vaasa Senate, the lateness of the withdrawal from Aunus in 1944 and aspects of his use of the general staff. But some important questions were left unasked or received only vague answers. Heinrichs acknowledged that Mannerheim was regarded as bearing a share of responsibility for Finland's involvement in the Continuation War but his account of the events of 1941 did not include a satisfactory evaluation of that responsibility. He was aware of Mannerheim's transformation from White General to Marshal of Finland but did not analyse it in detail. He did not discuss fully Mannerheim's attitude to democratic government. Nor did he have much to say about the Marshal's personality. In the epilogue to *The Marshal of Finland* Heinrichs emphasised the greatness of Mannerheim's decision to become commander-in-chief in 1939 and the unique confidence he enjoyed among all classes at the time of the armistice in 1944: absent from Finland for the best years of his life, he had returned to become one of its greatest sons and a central figure of the stormy first decades of independence.

A careful assessment of Mannerheim by Edwin Linkomies was published in *Oma maa* shortly before the appearance of Heinrichs' second volume.[53] Linkomies recognised the difficulty of describing Mannerheim because of the idealised picture of him dating from the War of Liberation and the admiration and hatred he then aroused, for equally subjective reasons, although it was not his fault the war had been a civil war. Linkomies repeated that Mannerheim had preserved his Finnish patriotic opinions while in Russia and had not adopted Russian attitudes. As regent, he had insufficient contact with parliament. Later developments had shown his interventionist policy to be mistaken militarily and politically and it was fortunate his advice had not been followed. Unlike Heinrichs, Linkomies attempted to compare Mannerheim's greatness with that of other Finns, concluding that although he was the most brilliant of Finland's great men, the foundations on which his career could be built had been laid by the philosopher Snellman and the poet Runeberg.

Yrjö Niiniluoto, editor of *Helsingin Sanomat*, recalled the comparison Linkomies made in a short but perceptive attempt to portray Mannerheim's character, published posthumously in 1962.[54] He thought it right to place Snellman before Mannerheim but considered that Runeberg and Mannerheim were not comparable. He added that, leaving aside the statesmen Svinhufvud and Ståhlberg, Öran Magnus Sprengtporten (1740–1819, who aimed to separate Finland from Sweden) and Klas Fleming (died 1597, who suppressed the Finnish peasant revolt of 1596–7) might also be compared with Mannerheim. Niiniluoto devoted more attention than previous writers to the significance of Mannerheim's years in Russia. He believed Russia had been Mannerheim's true environment, providing the atmosphere in which an elegant aristocrat could thrive. Mannerheim's sentimental attitude to the empire and his loyalty to Russia continued during and after the War of Liberation. Nevertheless, Niiniluoto also considered that Mannerheim had received a good basic knowledge of Finland from his family: unrussian in outlook and character, his most Russian feature was his cosmopolitanism. Although he had been a bystander in the struggle for Finland's rights, he could not avoid acknowledging those involved in that struggle after his return to Finland, and eventually referred to Russia as the hereditary enemy. Niiniluoto examined the Mannerheim cult, his character, reputation, role and greatness, and touched on personal topics that had hitherto been glossed over. Yet the emotive way he wrote of Mannerheim's undetermined place in history suggested that he was not wholly free from the influence of the Mannerheim myth himself.

An earlier attempt to describe Mannerheim's personality had been made by Yrjö Kivimies,[55] and the influence of the portrait he drew was apparent in what Heinrichs wrote about Mannerheim's character. Kivimies characterised Mannerheim as an aristocrat with a high moral sense of justice and as a *grand seigneur*. There was a vacuum round him, created by his personality, authority, age and, perhaps above all, his complete independence. Archibald Douglas had described Mannerheim as 'a man of honour without ambition'.[56] Kivimies agreed – Mannerheim was treated shamelessly but was always ready to serve though he had no greed for power. Niiniluoto recognised Mannerheim's ambition in 1918, and his description of him as a political general, but no dictator, was more accurate. Kivimies hoped to show Mannerheim's personality more clearly by presenting a collection of stories about him. This technique has been followed by others.[57] It lends itself more to piety than objectivity and is rarely helpful in elucidating the interplay of Mannerheim's character, ideas and actions.

The historian Juhani Paasivirta, in his studies of Finland during 1918 and 1919,[58] has provided an example of how information about Mannerheim's part in events can be linked to an analysis of his ideas and character so that they illustrate each other. He suggested why Mannerheim was so opposed to Bolshevism but not to Russia as such, explained how his career in Russia was partly responsible for his sympathies and manner of thinking, and showed how he was preoccupied by, and consistently pursued, a policy of intervention, considering the Finnish and Russian questions as one. Paasivirta distinguished the two parallel lines of thought vying for ascendency in Mannerheim's mind during 1919 – past vicissitudes and historical trends. As the result of his experiences he took on a new – or more properly a revived – Finnish nationalism and Finland's national interests began to hold in check the powerful crusading ambition brought about by his earlier experiences. Mannerheim's proud military nature made it a point of honour not to permit foreign intervention to reduce his share in the victory of 1918. But at the same time his realistic outlook enabled him to recognise German intervention in Finland as part of a wider German policy and oppose it as such. Paasivirta indicated how Mannerheim's attempt to become involved in the settlement of problems after the civil war aroused opposition because of his authoritarian character. In outlining the conflicts as well as the achievements of the regency, Paasivirta described how obviously distasteful to Mannerheim was the reform he had to bring about in Finnish domestic politics, and how even his nationalist supporters shunned his image as a 'general of intervention'.

The objective tone which pervades Paasivirta's work is totally lacking in the study by Arvi Nopanen of 'Carl Gustaf Emil Mannerheim to the year 1919'.[59] This book is the antithesis of the early encomiastic biographies although, perhaps surprisingly, Nopanen did not write from an extreme left-wing viewpoint. He considered Mannerheim's return in 1917 had been a disaster for Finland. Blind to his positive features and always attributing to him the worst possible motives, Nopanen branded Mannerheim as a military and political adventurer, totally alien to Finland and its people, whom he exploited ruthlessly and irresponsibly for the egoistical purpose of realising his dreams of greatness. Finland was saved from destruction when his interventionist policy, dictated by overriding interest in Russia, was frustrated. Mannerheim was set aside when his aspirations and character became known, and only then could the republic develop in peace. He and the nation had deceived themselves in believing that he was wise, upright and unselfish. However, as Nopanen stated, the earlier attitude to Mannerheim – the Mannerheim cult – had become less prevalent since the war and the unknown Mannerheim would become better known to the younger generation. Nopanen was right to expose some of the absurdities in the works of some of Mannerheim's admirers, though his obvious prejudice made his view of Mannerheim as suspect as theirs. Nevertheless, just as there was truth in the biographies which admired Mannerheim so uncritically, so there was truth, too, in Nopanen's book, and his criticisms should not be disregarded.

Mannerheim's strength of feeling for Russia, which had been glossed over by his Finnish admirers and so roundly condemned by Nopanen, had a positive side for Finland. Unlike the generations of Finns younger than himself, Mannerheim understood clearly the realities of the relationship between Finland and Russia and never supported a Finnish foreign policy rigorously antagonistic to Russian interests. This consequence of his very deep and persistent love for the old Russia was emphasised by Marvin Rintala, an American scholar, in a critical evaluation of Mannerheim's politics.[60] Mannerheim was anti-Bolshevik – as his 'large policy' of intervention in Russia in 1918–1919 proved – but never anti-Russian: he was always conciliatory towards legitimate or unavoidable Russian demands. In another work,[61] Rintala showed that the difference in the attitude towards Russia of the generations that matured politically before and after 1899 reflected the nature of the Russo-Finnish relationship during their formative years. Mannerheim, like other members of the older generation, had been brought up in a period of good relations between Finland and Russia and continued to believe in the possibility of co-operation with the imperial government after the period of oppression began in 1899. Rintala stressed that Mannerheim, whose political thought was as aristocratic as his personality, never accepted democracy. His leadership, when offered, was intensely personal. He regarded party activity as undisciplined, disruptive and selfish. His views were not totalitarian but pre-party and pre-democratic: this was a helpful insight by a historian and student of politics. Rintala concluded that Mannerheim's career in Finnish politics had been one frustrating crisis of mutual confidence after another, quite unlike his satisfying and successful career in Russia.

Rintala returned to the theme of Mannerheim's complete loyalty to imperial Russia before 1917 and complete devotion to it after the revolution in reviewing[62] the extremely important volumes by Stig Jägerskiöld about Mannerheim's early years and service in Russia.[63] Making use of much private family material not hitherto available to scholars, Jägerskiöld was able to describe Mannerheim's character, personality and background in such a way that they emerge with greater clarity and credibility than ever before: for the first time it has become possible to see Mannerheim as a human being rather than as a hero. Jägerskiöld's revelation of Mannerheim's struggle to succeed against powerful obstacles arouses admiration and even sympathy, particularly as he appears to have been a warm-hearted person, the favourite of his family, and not just an able and determined climber. Jägerskiöld concluded that Mannerheim's Finnish character was stamped on him before his career in Russia began, and that all through his service there he remained strongly attached to Finland, its traditions and the liberal-constitutionalist ideals of his family. 'The line from the Nikolayevskoye Cavalry School to the Finnish Headquarters, the Regency and finally the office of President has appeared uneven to many. In reality it was straight.'[64]

Mannerheim's assumption of the role of a Finnish leader was not accomplished without great difficulty on his part, but it would have been impossible had he become thoroughly russified. However, Jägerskiöld's placing of him in the Finnish constitutionalist tradition is open to doubt, particularly since his own material reveals that Mannerheim often acted and thought in ways contrary and even offensive, to Finnish constitutionalists. In spite of his continuing connections with Finland, the years in Russia modified Mannerheim's Finnish background to produce a highly individual outlook on politics and international affairs. He preserved a western way of thought about the state, but it was vastly different from the ideas of democratic government and party politics prevalent in Finland on his return. In addition, he had found in pre-revolutionary Russia a more congenial environment for the pursuit of his personal ideals than in Finland, either before or after independence. Rintala complained that Jägerskiöld did not grasp Mannerheim's complete loyalty to Russia. Nevertheless, it remains the great merit of Jägerskiöld's work that it has not only portrayed Mannerheim more clearly but has also provided the factual basis for a more informed discussion of his career, opinions and personality than has previously been possible.

Jägerskiöld's third volume continued his sympathetic and respectful account of Mannerheim's life from his return to Finland at the end of 1917 to his return to the country as regent the following year.[65] The source material for this period is rich and Jägerskiöld profited from the availability of contemporary diaries and letters and particularly of the British diplomatic papers. There is, however, less intimate detail of Mannerheim himself than was afforded by the extensive collections of family letters on which the earlier volumes were based. Jägerskiöld has material for many more volumes: a fourth is to describe Mannerheim in 1919.

Oliver Warner, a writer on English naval history, wrote a biography of Mannerheim to commemorate the centenary of the Marshal's birth.[66] Warner acknowledged that his treatment of events was at times partial and over-simplified. He relied greatly on Mannerheim's *Memoirs* and was an open admirer of his subject. He did not, however, hesitate to mention Mannerheim's political and military miscalculations and to acknowledge his weaknesses. The Marshal was characterised in Warner's book as a sophisticated soldier–statesman, an individualist, an authoritarian who nevertheless respected the rule of law. His affection was for the old, settled, pre-1914 Europe in which the masses had not yet made their influence felt. He believed they should be ruled with justice but denied them a share in government. Warner's book should dispel some of the prejudice surrounding Mannerheim by making him better known to the general reader in English-speaking countries. However, the need for more detailed study of Mannerheim in English remains.

The most recent Finnish work on Mannerheim was by the historian Matti Klinge.[67] The short essay that accompanied this pictorial biography reflected in several ways the new, scholarly approach to the study of Mannerheim. Klinge saw the beginning of the 'Mannerheim cult' in the early grey days of the republic, when Mannerheim represented glory and heroism. He showed how Mannerheim endeavoured not to prolong his role as the White General and how he gradually succeeded in his self-appointed task of recreating national unity. He pointed out that Mannerheim's political views and political activity in the 1920s and 1930s have not yet been made clear by research. Klinge was silent, however, about Mannerheim's role in the events of 1941, although work has been done on this period.

Kalle Lehmus entitled his recent book about the Marshal and the Second World War period 'The unknown Mannerheim'.[68] Mannerheim appeared in Finland in 1918 as an unknown Russian general. He remained essentially unknown not simply because he was withdrawn in nature and disapproved of observation of his private life, but because he became a symbol – for political and historical reasons – first of White Finland and later of national unity and independence. Quite apart from the general difficulty of writing objectively about recent events with the aid of only inadequate source material, his name stirred too many emotions for an impartial assessment of his character and role in Finnish history to be easy during his lifetime, and his admiring biographers scarcely made the attempt. The sensitivity resulting from Finland's defeat in 1944 affected comment about Mannerheim and other personalities involved in the events of the war period; this sensitivity has not entirely disappeared. However, it is becoming more possible for the historian to write usefully about Mannerheim as fresh material becomes available. In addition to literary sources, often in private hands, documentary sources in public archives are gradually being opened to researchers. The process of questioning and checking long-standing assumptions and assertions has begun and new interpretations are being put forward. The epithet 'unknown', long applicable to Mannerheim, is at last losing its validity.

REFERENCES

1. *Cf.* Edv. Hjelt, 'Finlands kamp för nationell frihet: historisk-politisk översikt', *Finlands frihetskrig skildrat av deltagare*, I, Helsingfors, 1921, p. 7.

2. [Allan Wallenius], *'Mannerheim den blodige' eller 'den vita djävulen'*, av Otto Grimlund [*pseud.*], Stockholm, 1919.

3. *Krasnaya gazeta*, 3 May, 1918, exclaimed 'Death to Kolchak and Mannerheim!' Quoted by Anatole G. Mazour, *Finland between East and West*, Princeton, 1956, p. 203.

4. One was displayed in the Mannerheim centenary exhibition at Helsinki University Library, *C. G. E. Mannerheim, 4.6.1867–4.6.1967*, exhibit no. 21. 'Butcher' was a term commonly used by the Reds about the Whites in general.

5. S. Smirnov, 'Neuklyuzhaya zateya reaktsiy', *Krasnaya zvezda*, Moskva, 2.vi.1967, p. 4.

6. *Suomen vapaussota vuonna 1918*, I, 2nd ed., Helsinki, 1922, p. vi.

7. Aarne Sihvo, *Muistelmani*, II, Helsinki, 1956, pp. 61–2.

8. *Suomen vapaussota vuonna 1918*, Helsinki, 1920–25, 6 vols.

9. *Suomen vapaussota*, Jyväskylä, 1921–28, 8 vols. The preface to this work recognised that the events it described were too close to be seen in perspective.

10. J. O. Hannula, *Suomen vapaussodan historia*, Porvoo, 1933. J. O. Hannula, *Finland's War of Independence*, London, 1939.

11. Hannes Ignatius, *Gustaf Mannerheim, luonnekuva, puheet, sähkösanomat vapaustaistelun ajoilta*, Helsinki, 1918.

12. Yrjö Koskelainen, *Mannerheim, Suomen vapauttaja ja valtionhoitaja. Mitä hän on sanonut ja mitä hänestä on sanottu*, Helsinki, 1919.

13. H. Ignatius, 'Kaarle Kustaa Eemil Mannerheim', *Oma maa*, III, 2nd ed., Porvoo, 1922, pp. 659–69.

14. Kai Donner, *Sotamarsalkka vapaaherra Mannerheim*, Porvoo, 1934.

15. Juhani Paasivirta, *Suomi vuonna 1918*, Porvoo, 1957, p. 377.

16. Donner, *Sotamarsalkka vapaaherra Mannerheim*, p. [iii].

17. Kai Donner, 'Mannerheim, Karl Gustaf Emil', *Kansallinen elämäkerrasto*, IV, Porvoo, 1932, pp. 11–20.

18. Donner, *Sotamarsalkka vapaaherra Mannerheim*, p. [iii].

19. C. G. Mannerheim, *Across Asia from West to East in 1906–1908*, Helsinki, 1940, 2 vols.

20. C. G. Mannerheim, *Resa genom Asien. Fältmarskalken C. G. Mannerheims dagbok förda under hans resa Kaspiska havet – Peking*, Stockholm, 1940, 2 vols. Abridged Swedish editions appeared in 1942 and 1961: C. G. Mannerheim, *Till häst genom Asien. Förkortad upplaga redigerad av Kaarlo Hildén*, Helsingfors, 1942; C. G. Mannerheim, *Till häst genom Asien. Redigerad och med inledning av Göran Schildt*, Helsingfors, 1961. C. G. Mannerheim, *Matka Aasian halki; päiväkirja matkalta Kaspianmeri – Peking*, Helsinki, 1940, 41, 2 vols. C. G. Mannerheim, *Fra Samarkand til Peking paa hesteryg*, København, 1941. C. G. Mannerheim, *Rit door Azië*, Amsterdam, 1943.

21. Stig Jägerskiöld, *Gustaf Mannerheim, 1906–1917*, Helsingfors, 1965.

22. *C. G. Mannerheim*. Toim. H. Kekoni ja H. J. Viherjuuri, Helsinki, 1937.

23. W. E. Tuompo, 'Sotilas ja sotapäällikkö', *C. G. Mannerheim*, Helsinki, 1937, p. 139.

24. *Kesäkuun neljäs päivä 1942; Suomen marsalkan, vapaaherra C. G. Mannerheimin 75-vuotispäivän juhlallisuudet*, Helsinki, 1942. *Sotamarsalkka Mannerheim 75 vuotta kesäkuun 4 päivänä 1942. Juhlajulkaisu*, Helsinki, 1942. *C. G. Mannerheim, Suomen marsalkka*, Helsinki, Kivi, 1951. *Marskalken av Finland, friherre Gustaf Mannerheim; krigaren, statsmannen, människan*, Helsingfors, 1953.

25. Kai Donner, *Feltmarskal friherre Mannerheim*, København, 1940.

26. Kai Donner, and Georg Wasmuth Sejersted, *Feltmarskalk Mannerheim*, Oslo, 1941.

27. C. de Bourcet, *Le baron Mannerheim, maréchal de Finlande*, Paris, 1940.

28. János Kósa, *Mannerheim tábornagy*, Budapest, 1940.

29. Tancred Borenius, *Field-Marshal Mannerheim*, London, 1940. Paul Rodzyanko, *Mannerheim: an Intimate Picture of a Great Soldier and Statesman*, London, 1940. A bio-

graphy in German was published significantly later: August Beranek, *Mannerheim*, Berlin, 1942. Mannerheim's life was interpreted by Beranek against the background of the war between Germany and the Soviet Union and a chapter on his interventionist policy in 1919 was entitled 'Erzfeind des Bolschewismus',

30. Borenius, *Field-Marshal Mannerheim*, pp. vii–viii.

31. Rodzyanko, *Mannerheim*, p. 97.

32. Stig Jägerskiöld, *Den unge Mannerheim*, Helsingfors, 1964, p. 7.

33. J. O. Hannula, *Mannerheim; vapaussodan ylipäällikkö*, Helsinki, 1937.

34. Anni Voipio, *Suomen sotamarsalkka*, Porvoo, 1942. Anni Voipio, *Suomen marsalkka; elämäkerta*, 5th ed., Porvoo, 1952.

35. Voipio, *Suomen marsalkka*, 3rd ed., Porvoo, 1951, pp. 5–6.

36. John I. Kolehmainen, 'The memoirs of Marshal Mannerheim', *American historical review*, 60, New York, 1955, pp. 429–30.

37. G. Mannerheim, *Minnen*, Helsingfors, 1951–52, 2 vols. G. Mannerheim, *Muistelmatl* Helsinki, 1951–52, 2 vols.

38. *The Memoirs of Marshal Mannerheim*, London, 1953; *Les mémoires du marécha*, *Mannerheim, 1882–1946*, Paris, 1952; G. Mannerheim, *Erinnerungen*, Zürich, 1952; *Mariscal Mannerheim: memorias*, Barcelona, 1954.

39. Arvi Korhonen, 'Suomen marsalkka muistelmakirjailijana', *Suomalainen Suomi*, 20, Helsinki, 1952, p. 266.

40. Arvi Korhonen, *Barbarossa-suunnitelma ja Suomi; jatkosodan synty*, Porvoo, 1961, p. 25.

41. Onni Talas, *Suomen itsenäistyminen ja Mannerheimin muistelmat*, Hämeenlinna, 1953.

42. Kolehmainen, 'The Memoirs of Marshal Mannerheim', pp. 429–30.

43. C. Leonard Lundin, *Finland in the Second World War*, Bloomington, 1957, p. 255.

44. Arvi Korhonen, *Barbarossa-suunnitelma ja Suomi; jatkosodan synty*, Porvoo, 1961.

45. Gustaf Ehrnrooth, 'Carl Gustaf Emil Mannerheim (1867–1951); minnestal', *Marskalken av Finland, friherre Gustaf Mannerheim; krigaren, statsmannen, människan*, Helsingfors, 1953, p. 26.

46. *Cf.* Edwin Linkomies, 'C. G. Mannerheim', *Oma maa*, VI, Porvoo, 1959, pp. 44–57.

47. A. F. Upton, *Finland in crisis, 1940–1941: a study in small-power politics*, London, 1964.

48. For example, the review by S. J., 'Uptonin kriisi', *Suomalainen Suomi*, 33, Helsinki, 1965, pp. 445–6. It was asked whether the allied leaders had always acted democratically.

49. *Marskalken av Finland, friherre Gustaf Mannerheim; krigaren, statsmannen, människan*, Helsingfors, 1953, p. 7.

50. Erik Heinrichs, 'Mannerheim som överbefälhavare,' *Marskalken av Finland, riherre Gustaf Mannerhe im; krigaren, statsmannen, människan*, Helsingfors, 1953, pp. 45–56.

51. Erik Heinrichs, *Mannerheim Suomen kohtaloissa*, Helsinki, 1957, 59, 2 vols.

52. Heinrichs, *Mannerheim Suomen kohtaloissa*, i. p. 17.

53. Edwin Linkomies, 'C. G. Mannerheim', *Oma maa*, VI, Porvoo, 1959, pp. 44–57.

54. Yrjö Niiniluoto, *Suuri rooli; Suomen marsalkan, vapaaherra Carl Gustaf Emil Mannerheimin kirjallisen muotokuvan yritelmä*, Helsinki, 1962.

55. Yrjö Kivimies, *Suomen marsalkka tuokiokuvina*, Helsinki, 1951.

56. Archibald Douglas, 'Mannerheim', *Svensk tidskrift*, 38, Uppsala, 1951, p. 76.

57. *Marski läheltä ja kaukaa*, Helsinki, 1964. Matti Kurjensaari, 'G. Mannerheim,

1944–1946', *Presidenttikaskut; kaskuja ja tarinoita tasavallan kahdeksasta päämiehestä,* Tampere, 1961, pp. 72–90.

58. Juhani Paasivirta, *Suomi vuonna 1918,* Porvoo, 1957., Juhani Paasivirta, *The victors in World War I and Finland,* Helsinki, 1965. The original was: *Ensimmäisen maailmansodan voittajat ja Suomi,* Porvoo, 1961.

59. Arvi Nopanen, *Carl Gustaf Emil Mannerheim vuoteen 1919 saakka,* Lahti, 1963.

60. Marvin Rintala, 'The politics of Gustaf Mannerheim', *Journal of Central European Affairs,* 21, Boulder, 1961, pp. 67–83. A later version of this article appears in Marvin Rintala, *Four Finns: political profiles,* Berkeley, 1969, pp. 13–46.

61. Marvin Rintala, *Three generations: the extreme right wing in Finnish politics,* Bloomington, 1962.

62. Marvin Rintala, 'Stig Jägerskiöld. Nuori Mannerheim', *Russian review,* 24, New York, 1965, pp. 300–1; 'Stig Jägerskiöld. Gustaf Mannerheim, 1906–1917', *ibid.,* 25, 1966, pp. 314–5.

63. Stig Jägerskiöld, *Den unge Mannerheim,* Helsingfors, 1964. Stig Jägerskiöld, *Gustaf Mannerheim, 1906–1917,* Helsingfors, 1965.

64. Jägerskiold, *Gustaf Mannerheim,* p. 339.

65. Stig Jägerskiöld, *Gustaf Mannerheim, 1918,* Helsingfors, 1967.

66. Oliver Warner, *Marshal Mannerheim and the Finns,* London, 1967.

67. Matti Klinge, *Mannerheim; kuvaelämäkerta,* Helsinki, 1968.

68. Kalle Lehmus, *Tuntematon Mannerheim: katkelmia sodan ja politiikan poluilta,* Helsinki, 1967.

CHAPTER I

FORMATIVE YEARS

4ᴱ June 1867

Baron Carl Gustaf Emil Mannerheim, Marshal of Finland, was born on 4 June, 1867, at his family's estate of Louhisaari in south-western Finland.[1] Louhisaari, at Askainen about twenty miles from Turku, had been bought by his great-grandfather when he left Sweden to settle in Finland at the end of the eighteenth century. The Marshal's Swedish ancestors had risen from obscurity to high rank in four generations. Their progress from merchant and banker to civil servant, from landowner to soldier and high state official was not exceptional, particularly in eighteenth-century Sweden where the aristocracy of bureaucrats, soldiers and sailors never became a closed caste. The founder of the family, Henrik Marhein, was Dutch, but he came to Sweden from Germany. The name of Mannerheim was adopted by his youngest son Augustin when he was ennobled in 1693 by Charles XI of Sweden. Augustin's sons became soldiers and two of them were raised to the rank of baron. The younger baron, Johan Augustin, was the father of Carl Erik Mannerheim who bought Louhisaari and founded the Finnish branch of the family.[2]

Carl Erik Mannerheim became a member of the Finnish government after the Russian invasion of 1808 and the subsequent acknowledgment of the Emperor as Grand Duke of Finland. In 1824 he was made a count: this title was to be transmitted by primogeniture, other sons retaining the title of baron. The second count, Carl Gustaf, the Marshal's grandfather, was the first member of the family to be born in Finland. Like his father he entered the government service and eventually became president of the court of appeal at Viipuri, though he achieved greater fame as an entomologist. His son, Count Carl Robert Mannerheim, father of the Marshal, departed from family tradition in adopting a radical political outlook and in becoming neither soldier nor administrator. Succeeding his father while still an undergraduate, with a reputation as the author of political satires objectionable to the authorities, he was able to indulge his literary inclinations and write and translate poetry. But business activities played an increasingly important part in his life after his marriage in 1862 to Hedvig Charlotta Helena von Julin, known as Hélène, the daughter of a prominent and well-connected Finnish industrialist, Johan Jakob von Julin.

Count and Countess Mannerheim had seven children, four boys and three girls, all born between 1863 and 1873: the third child and second son, Gustaf, was the future Marshal of Finland. Hélène Mannerheim was the centre of the world of Louhisaari, where she brought up her children in an atmosphere remarkable for its dignified formality. The style of life at home reflected the influence of her husband's aristocratic background rather than his political radicalism. His liberal ideals, and consciousness of Finland's western political and constitutional traditions, nevertheless communicated themselves to his family. This background, together with his intimate contact with the literary and art world, produced a cultured environment that was to exert a quiet but strong influence on Gustaf. Hélène's kindness and understanding were tempered by a rather spartan simplicity since she realised the importance of a strong physique and tried to harden her young family by means of cold baths and horsehair mattresses. But this apparent austerity did not spoil the happiness of the children, who were in their element in the exciting playground of the estate and its surroundings.

Louhisaari was undoubtedly one of the finest estates in Finland. It was noted particularly for the long avenue of birch trees extending from the church of Askainen to the house, for its park, and for the gardens that were laid out in English style with ornamental ponds and winding paths. The manor house itself, 'a simple but imposing granite cube, with three floors, and a steep pyramidal roof with mansard windows,' was already old when rebuilt by the Fleming family in the seventeenth century.[3] Its interior was richly decorated with wall and ceiling paintings, some of them depicting the victories of Admiral Klas Fleming. One of the bedrooms was held in special awe by the children because the mural included a painting of the devil. The sea, which was visible from the back of the house only a short distance beyond the trees of the park and the cornfields, was the object of many excursions, the youngsters playing happily on the beach in their thick woollen costumes, or rowing or sailing in the archipelago. The delightful country life of Louhisaari was varied only by equally pleasurable visits to the estates of numerous relatives and friends in south-west Finland.

19

The children got on well together, though Gustaf and Carl, his eldest brother, were constant rivals who eagerly organised the others and any visiting cousins into two opposing private armies. Johan was Gustaf's best ally; they shared an enthusiasm for horses and riding that remained a life-long bond between them. Sophie, the eldest of the family, was a responsible girl who became entrusted more and more with the care of the younger ones, Eva, Anna and August. In the course of time a very close relationship developed between her and Gustaf, whose clear-cut views and strong and upright character were so similar to her own, and were perhaps to some extent moulded by them. But the self-discipline and sense of duty characteristic of Mannerheim's maturity contrast sharply with the wildness of his boyhood. Although backward in learning to talk, Gustaf was far from backward at getting into trouble. He was attracted irresistibly to adventure and danger. He fell into lakes, roamed away on his own, and injured himself when he fell whilst attempting to jump across the roof beams of a new cow-shed. His attitude as well as his activities greatly worried his mother, who blamed the nurses for spoiling 'his lively, happy and frank spirit'.[4] She complained to her sister: 'I have much trouble from Gustaf, whose unbridled and boisterous nature does not change . . . Certainly he could still improve but his example influences the younger children and disturbs the peace of the house.'[5] Count Mannerheim was away a great deal on business connected with the Kuusankoski Paper Company he had founded, and it was not surprising that his return usually meant a good beating for Gustaf and his brothers.

Young Mannerheim's pranks were not compensated by any enthusiasm for learning, a fact lamented by his mother when he was only five. In the autumn of 1875 he entered the preparatory school of the Private Lyceum in Helsinki, a distinguished boys' school near the Kaisaniemi park, which his father had attended before him. His brother Carl entered the main school at the same time, the boys living with their father in a flat in Helsinki. Two years later, when Johan joined his brothers at school, the whole family moved to the capital for the winter. Gustaf, who more than held his own in the rough and tumble of school life, acquired a reputation as a dare-devil and a practical joker. At the age of seven he wrote confidentially to his sister Sophie that the boys nicknamed him the wild buck and the girls called him 'patron mannagryn'.[6] He often fought with boys bigger than himself and was undisputed leader of his class in snowball fights in Kaisaniemi park. There is a story that on one occasion, when paying more attention to the 'enemy' than the traffic, he was run

1875

over by a horse-drawn sleigh. However, he got up unhurt and threw his last snowball defiantly, explaining afterwards to anxious bystanders: 'My name is Mannerheim, and I am the general of the lower form'.[7]

He was a puzzle to his teachers, and in March 1879 the headmaster called on Countess Mannerheim to say that he had expelled Gustaf for deliberately breaking windows. She thought the punishment 'severe . . . though legitimate', and took him away to Louhisaari where he was 'much more easy to handle alone'. His future caused her constant concern. Finally she thought he might make a soldier: the discipline would surely do him good. 'I intend to discuss with him whether he would attempt the entrance examination to the cadet school in the spring, though I know that he is averse to going into the Russian army. . . . He is so absolutely pro-Swedish.'[8] Both sides of his family had relatives living in Sweden, and the von Julins in particular had established strong connections with the country. He certainly regarded Sweden with affection, and retained his concern for it throughout his life. It is more likely, however, that his mother used the word Swedish to mean that he was loyal to the traditions of the Swedish-speaking Finns.[9] Perhaps his boundless disappointment at the surrender of Osman Pasha during the Russo-Turkish War of 1877-78 had led her to believe he was anti-Russian. In fact, he had as yet no desire whatsoever to become a soldier – his inclinations were towards music and literature, especially history. However, his deep attachment to his mother evidently led him to follow her suggestion, which she might not have been so anxious to press on him had not the reduced financial circumstances of the family made it necessary to cut the cost of his education.

The cadet school to which Countess Mannerheim referred was the Corps of Cadets, a boarding school at Hamina which traced its origins back to the last decades of Swedish rule in Finland, and was the only establishment for military education in the country. 'This fine, honourable institution, with its homogeneous body of pupils, for the most part recruited from good, educated, patriotic homes, its mode of life almost Spartan in its severity and power to harden, its proud, upright spirit',[10] had a good reputation, and competition for places there was keen. The course of instruction lasted seven years; a preparatory year followed by three years of general classes and three of special classes for those aspiring to commissions. Some cadets chose to follow civilian careers and left after only four years, but most remained. The majority of those who became officers had to enter the Russian army until the Army Law of

1878 created a Finnish national militia and provided more opportunities for them at home. Gustaf Mannerheim was sent to school at Hamina in 1880 to prepare for the entrance examination, but failed to get into the appropriate class and lost the chance of entering the Corps of Cadets in 1881. Money had to be found for the expenses of another year, which was no easy matter. Despite the report of his landlady – a distant connection on the von Julin side – that he was possessed of considerable powers of comprehension, his mother did not believe he had a hope of success unless he improved, and became very worried when he again got into trouble for misbehaviour.[11]

As has been intimated, Countess Mannerheim had other worries besides Gustaf. Her earnest and deeply Christian character was pained by her husband's lack of tenacity and indifference to religion, and she had to watch helplessly while his inability to resist the lure of gambling – until it was too late – led to the family's financial ruin. By 1879 the pressure of his debts forced him to sell the estate of Hannula adjoining Louhisaari. His fitful interest in agriculture waned as he devoted his restless mind to other things, and his own economic position and that of Louhisaari became so bad that it, too, had to be sold to help settle his affairs when he eventually went bankrupt in 1880 and relatives and friends tried to clear up his chaotic finances. He had already left his family homeless and penniless and gone abroad with his mistress. Countess Mannerheim had no alternative but to go to her stepmother's home at Sällvik. Her health was failing and she suffered severe pain: she had a heart attack, and on 23 January, 1881, she died. Count Mannerheim came home for the funeral, and then returned to Paris and his mistress, whom he later married. His sister, Wilhelmina, became the new owner of Louhisaari and took care of the two youngest girls. Carl and Gustaf sometimes stayed with her and with their grandmother, Countess Eva Mannerheim, during their holidays, but it was their mother's brother, Albert von Julin, who assumed responsibility for Gustaf.

The death of their mother and the dispersal of the family among various relatives in Finland and Sweden marked the end of the innocent days of childhood. It was a tragedy above all for Gustaf, who had been very fond of his mother. She had appreciated his good qualities and recognised the difficulty he experienced in trying to force the temperamental and often aggressive side of his nature to conform to the demands of authority, a problem that was exacerbated by the family disaster and became even more acute during the next few years.

The difficulties of Gustaf's future were apparently resolved in 1882 when he was at last admitted to the Corps of Cadets. The long-awaited improvement in his work had begun to take place. However, he was left in the Preparatory Class for a second year after consideration of the examination results in June 1883, when he averaged only 7 out of 12, but he profited from the extra year by becoming top of the class in December 1883 and was moved up to the First General Class in second place six months later. He did particulary well at French, Swedish and History, less well at Russian and Finnish. As befitted the grandson of an ento-mologist, he was quite good at Natural History, and his improvement in science subjects was commended in June 1884. His average became 9·2 in 1884 and 9·3 in 1885;[12] he was undoubtedly gifted, and secured a free place.

Although there was an excellent spirit among the cadets and he was quickly acknowledged as a leader by his contemporaries, this first taste of military life was not to his liking. He found communal living unpleasant. His aesthetic interests were not shared by his fellow-cadets and he missed the cultured atmosphere in which he had been brought up. The town of Hamina itself was depressing, and he certainly resented being sent there as the victim of his family's impoverishment. He was always humiliatingly short of money, and at one point ran up a considerable debt which he finally had to confess with shame to his Uncle Albert. Deeply disturbed to receive evidence of his nephew's apparent folly in money matters – feared to be an inheritance from Count Mannerheim – Uncle Albert treated him to a lecture on the virtues of thrift and sober acquaintance, but with characteristic generosity sent the money Gustaf needed, much to his relief and gratitude. Such reminders of his dependence, accompanied usually by exhortations to work hard, though prompted by kindness and concern, cannot have been pleasant. Nor was daily life at the school attractive. Food was poor and comforts were few. The routine was monotonous. Years later, he felt that the remoteness of Finland and the small size of the Finnish army had an adverse effect on the military training the school offered. Promotion of the instructors was slow and some of them were eccentric characters. However, the military atmosphere improved after Major-General Carl Enckell succeeded Major-General Frithiof Alfred Neovius as Director in November 1885, and tightened up still further the already strict discipline.

Independent, obstinate, and accustomed to a less regimented existence, Mannerheim found many of the petty regulations irksome and became involved in a constant battle with the authorities, seldom committing a serious offence, but incurring repeated punishment. Detention for varying periods of time on Sundays followed such boyish offences as inattention, whispering, noisiness, laziness, and occasionally cribbing. The dancing lessons evidently attracted his especial derision. On different occasions he was punished for talking and noise, undue laughter and unruliness during the dancing lesson. In March 1884 he claimed he was unfit to dance because of a boil, but managed to go to a gymnastics lesson later the same day, an inconsistency that cost him his leave for a whole weekend. A similarly severe punishment was ordered by the Director in December after he had hit a younger cadet. His conduct marks never rose above 6 – some of his contemporaries secured 8 – and fell to 4 in December 1884.[13]

The environment of Hamina was certainly uncongenial to him and it was not surprising that he tried to get away. He wrote to his sister Sophie on 16 February, 1884: 'It is as disagreeable here as usual, vexation after vexation. I look forward with joy to the moment when I can turn my back on Finland for ever and go my own way – God knows where, but in any case my own master.'[14] His thoughts were turning to the possibility of a military career in Russia, which would be all the more attractive if he could avoid a regiment buried in some provincial town. The disaster that had overwhelmed his happy childhood had thus brought about a complete change in his outlook as well as in his circumstances. In 1879 his mother had thought him averse to going into the Russian army: after two years at the Corps of Cadets he had become keen to obtain a military education at the School of Pages in St. Petersburg and get a commission in a Russian regiment. It is significant that his dissatisfaction was with his economic dependence, with the Corps of Cadets, even with Finland, but no longer with military service as such. By this time he had accepted that the army was to be his career.

Ever since Finland had come under Russian rule in 1809 – and, indeed, even before that – small numbers of Finns, especially members of the nobility, including some connected with Mannerheim's family, had entered the Russian service and a few had risen to high rank. 'Their puritanical honor, their conscientious attitude towards their obligations' won them high regard as 'to the highest degree useful laborers and assistants in all branches of military service.'[15] It was not thought strange that they should go to Russia. The Emperor was their sovereign as Grand Duke of Finland and relations between the two realms were excellent for the greater part of the nineteenth century. In Russia they were challenged by a world entirely different from the provincial Finnish scene, in which the opportunities for an ambitious man were incomparably greater than in Finland, but where the struggle to succeed was correspondingly keener. Many who stayed at home even held it to be of the utmost importance that there should be Finns well-known in Russia who had retained their loyalty to their native country and whom the Emperor could appoint to high posts in the Finnish administration.[16] Finns who were acquainted with Russian conditions and the Russian language acted as necessary intermediaries between the two countries in civil, military and economic affairs, and prevented the development of a group of immigrant Russians to perform the same task.[17] The favourable aspects of service in Russia would be readily apparent to a boy at the Corps of Cadets, and Mannerheim was aware, too, that he inherited a tradition of serving the Emperor in Russia as well as in Finland.

There were, however, Finns who were suspicious of service in the autocratic empire. They recalled with concern that while some Finns who served in Russia had retained their Finnish outlook, others had become assimilated in the Russian military and official class and did not hesitate to implement Russian policies inimical to Finnish interests. Because of this, it was felt by many Finns, especially those who watched anxiously over Finland's autonomous constitutional position, that service in the empire was undesirable, even wrong: this attitude was widespread among industrialists and landowners like von Julins and their connections in south-west Finland; it was shared by Count Carl Robert Mannerheim; it prevailed, too, among young people in Helsinki, like Carl Mannerheim and his friends.

Even in the 1880s, when it might have appeared difficult to sustain serious patriotic and political objections to Mannerheim's desire to go to Russia, he found it hard to win the approval of his von Julin relatives for his plans. His aunt, Hanna Lovén, believed his wish to transfer to the School of Pages was the result of the influence of the Mannerheims. Lack of money made the financial support of his uncle Albert von Julin essential, and the attitude of this kindly but cautious man was decisive. He hesitated over the cost of the project and the risk that his nephew might become russified. Mannerheim argued the advantages of tranferring from the Corps of Cadets to the Imperial School of Pages in St. Petersburg and proceeding as soon as possible to the General Staff Academy. From the School of Pages it would be relatively easy to get into a good regiment in Russia and continue to the Academy, by which time he would be able to start repaying the debts he would incur during his first years' service. He would not be faced with the likelihood of a long wait, as an unpaid supernumerary officer, for a vacancy in a Finnish regiment. To pass through the General Staff Academy was practically a guarantee of a successful career. The majority of higher commands were occupied by general staff officers; the remainder usually went to officers from the guards. Later on, Mannerheim tried to persuade his uncle of the advantages of combining both ways to achieve success by joining a guards regiment first and then going to the Academy. He believed his work was sufficiently good for him to be accepted at the School of Pages, and also that he would be able to reduce the expense involved by obtaining a grant from the state. Despite the reluctance of Uncle Albert he went ahead with his plans.

Although critical towards Russia in general and its army in particular, Count Carl Robert Mannerheim wrote to the acting Minister-Secretary of State for Finland in St. Petersburg in September 1884, asking if his son could be considered for one of the free places reserved for Finns at the School of Pages.[18] This was 'the most privileged military training institution in Russia', admitting only members of the hereditary nobility whose fathers, grandfathers or great-grandfathers had held at least the rank of lieutenant-general, or its civilian equivalent.[19] Count Mannerheim's own rank did not entitle him to ask this favour, but he did so in consideration of that of his father and grandfather. It was recognised that those who passed through the Imperial School of Pages generally had a brilliant future ahead of them, and therein lay its attraction. To Mannerheim, the School offered the means to escape from his present unhappy existence into a grander and more exciting world.

The request was referred to the head of the Corps of Cadets, Major-General Neovius, whose recommendation was necessary before the transfer could be initiated. It met with an exceptionally abrupt refusal on the grounds that Mannerheim's knowledge of Russian and French was insufficient, but his unsatisfactory conduct was the real reason Neovius was not prepared to follow the normal procedure and let an entrance examination be arranged for him. When his grandmother, Countess Eva Mannerheim, renewed the request in October 1885 she was told the places for that year had been already filled. She wrote to the Minister-Secretary of State again in March 1886, anxious to be able to tell her grandson how the matter was progressing, and fearing that an unfavourable decision would upset not only his future but his whole desire and ability to work. The reply merely quoted Neovius' negative report of 1884, and added that Mannerheim now exceeded the age limit for entrance to the Imperial School of Pages, though no attempt had been made to ask whether the limit would be rigorously applied in such a case. Mannerheim had been confident of a recommendation since he had secured an increased conduct mark, and was bitterly disappointed by the unfairness of Neovius' decision and the failure to get away from the oppressive atmosphere of the Corps of Cadets. There was nothing more the family could do, and he seemed fated to serve in the Finnish army with its circumscribed opportunities.

His grandmother's fears of the psychological consequences of the disappointment were justified. His conduct deteriorated. He was confined to barracks until further notice, by order of the Director, for going out without permission one evening in April 1885. The autumn brought detention for unruliness, muttering in class and attempted cribbing. Finally he was roused to more serious rebellion. In the evening of Good Friday, 23 April, 1886, he took French leave, arranging a dummy in his bed, and going first to an inn and then to the house of a friend in the country. The Sergeant-Major of the Corps got to hear of this and brought him back on Saturday morning. The Education Committee of the Corps met that day to decide what to do. The Director moved that he should be expelled, since he had already committed many serious offences and had a bad influence on the other cadets. The committee agreed to the proposal, though it voted not to apply the regulation about expulsion in full, but to ask Mannerheim's guardian to put in a request for his resignation. He had to leave at once.[20]

The expulsion was a serious blow which threw open the whole question of his future. Uncle Albert hoped he would take the matriculation examination and then follow a civilian career in Finland, but Mannerheim still favoured service in Russia and wanted more than anything else to become a naval officer. The sea fascinated him during his early years, and its attraction had been increased by the example of his famous uncle, the sailor and explorer Adolf Erik Nordenskiöld,[21] and by the service of distant relatives in the imperial navy. Hopes of achieving this aim were dashed, however, because a good conduct certificate from the Corps of Cadets was a prerequisite for his entering the naval cadet school in St. Petersburg. Uncle Albert suggested he went to stay with his brother-in-law, Edvard Bergenheim, who ran a factory in Kharkov: the visit would give him chance to see something of the country, improve his Russian, and think over his plans for the future. He spent the summer of 1886 at Kharkov and at a military camp nearby at Chuguchev, where his Russian tutor, a Captain, was stationed. Life in the garrison – more servitude than grandeur – was depressing and shook somewhat his preconceived ideas of the Russian army, although he commented that he had nothing against the military life and would not hesitate to be a soldier if he had the money. He had considered taking the entrance examination to the Nikolayevskoye Cavalry School in St. Petersburg in the autumn of 1887 but returned to Finland in October 1886 apparently bent on a civil career. He was able to go back to the Private Lyceum to study for the matriculation examination.

On 14 June, 1887, after a year of hard work interrupted by an attack of typhoid fever, he passed the examination, with a good result, and became a student at the University of Helsinki, enrolling in the Historical-Philological Department of the Faculty of Arts.[22] A school friend wrote of him: 'Little was left of the dare-devil. He was a steady and mature young man with a lively intellect, remarkably sure, urbane and realistic in behaviour, and a good comrade, too.'[23] The expulsion from the Corps of Cadets, which he always regarded as a great injustice, had made a deep impression on him, and the psychological consequences of his recklessness were salutary. He wrote in his *Memoirs*: 'My disciplinary punishment had spurred my ambition to show that, despite this unfortunate prank, I was at heart a good soldier.'[24]

He had realised that the army was his true calling and, although he had matriculated, had no intention of going to the university. The military way of life offered an outlet for his desire to lead and capacity for leadership, his eagerness for adventure and willingness to work hard. With its emphasis on action, its glamour, its encouragement of riding and field sports, which he loved, and the companionship of like-minded men in an ordered society, the army was to appeal increasingly to his interests and temperament. He had learned the importance of self-control, to regulate his enthusiasm and to accept discipline; having done so, he became a responsible leader, and in time a strict disciplinarian. The matriculation was the qualification for entry to Russian officer cadet schools and freed him from the need to refer to his time at the Corps of Cadets and the reason he left there.[25] Not surprisingly, thought of a civilian career was now abandoned.

He had determined to be a cavalry officer, a natural choice for one so fond of horses, though he was also influenced by the wretched reputation of the infantry, and decided to implement his earlier plan to go to the Nikolayevskoye Cavalry School, the most satisfactory way of training for a commission in a cavalry regiment. He made energetic use of his contacts to secure a place there. One of his godmothers, Louise Cedercreutz, was married to the then Major-General Baron Gösta Aminoff, who agreed to try to help him. Louise's sister Alfhild, who had married Mikhail Petrovich Scalon de Coligny, was also godmother to Mannerheim, and invited him to stay at their estate at Lukianovka near Kursk during the summer. He spent a delightful month there, and before moving on to study at Kharkov and Chuguchev secured the valuable patronage of the eminent Scalon family. In July he heard the good news that Aminoff had succeeded in obtaining a vacancy for him at the Nikolayevskoye Cavalry School through his connection with General Bilderling, the School's head. Mannerheim's gratitude was profound, though he worried whether his knowledge of Russian would be sufficient to enable him to pass the entrance examination in August. His fears proved unfounded; he passed easily and was accepted.

After a farewell dinner with his friends from the Private Lyceum at which he promised never to forget Finland, he left for St. Petersburg in the autumn of 1887. His decision to go to Russia, although he was merely following the example of many respected members of the Finnish nobility, caused his relatives much heart-searching, and he was sufficiently conscious, if heedless, of their liberal and deeply patriotic objections to his plans to write them an ironical letter of farewell from St. Petersburg, in which he signed himself 'Gustaf, the apostate'.[26] Expulsion from the Corps of Cadets, which precluded the possibility of a military career in Finland, took on a new significance: it had enabled him to follow his original inclination to escape from Finland and to serve in Russia.

1887

REFERENCES

1. The Swedish name is Villnäs. Louhisaari is described in Riitta Pylkkänen and Per-Olof Westlin, *Louhisaari Villnäs*, Porvoo, 1968.

2. On Mannerheim's family and ancestors see the articles by Bruno Lesch and Osmo Durchman in *C. G. Mannerheim*. Toim. H. Kekoni ja H. J. Viherjuuri, Helsinki, 1937.

3. Borenius, *Field-Marshal Mannerheim*, p. 12.

4. Eva Mannerheim Sparre, *Lapsuuden muistoja*, Helsinki, 1952, p. 15.

5. Mannerheim Sparre, *Lapsuuden muistoja*, pp. 14–15.

6. Jägerskiöld, *Den unge Mannerheim*, p. 32. Lit. 'master manna (semolina) groats'.

7. Borenius, *Field-Marshal Mannerheim*, p. 14. This story is typical of many, of varying degrees of accuracy, told about Mannerheim at different periods of his life, but with the common characteristic of exemplifying some attribute desirable in a great man.

8. Mannerheim Sparre, *Lapsuuden muistoja*, pp. 70-3.

9. An example of the use of the word 'Swedish' in this sense is quoted by Anders Mattson Myhrman, *The Swedish Nationality Movement in Finland*, Chicago, 1939, pp. 58-9: 'My home was very Swedish, We spoke the Swedish language and read Swedish authors, played Swedish music, danced Swedish dances. When I say "Swedish" I do not necessarily mean that all this had been directly imported from Sweden; much of it had been written on Finnish soil by men and women born in Finland. What I want to emphasize is that my upbringing was thoroughly Swedish.'

10. G. M. Nordenswan, 'Pojkminnen från gamla Kadettkåren', *Finsk tidskrift*, 147, Helsingfors, 1950, p. 129.

11. Mannerheim Sparre, *Lapsuuden muistoja*, p. 78.

12. Sota-arkisto. [SA]. M. 279. Finska Kadettkåren. *Attestationshäften för kadetterna.* Barona Mannerkheima. M. 276. *Uppfostrings komiténs protokoll bok*, 1871-1887. Entries for 14 Juni 1883, 13 Juni 1884.

13. SA. M. 275. *Kadetternas straff journal, 1880-1885*, M. 276. *Protokoll bok.*

14. Jägerskiöld, *Den unge Mannerheim*, p. 64.

15. J. S. Curtiss, *The Russian Army under Nicholas I, 1825-1855*. Durham, NC, 1965, p. 207, quoting A. L. Zisserman, *Dvadtsat pyat let na Kavkaze (1842-1867)*, S.-Peterburg, 1879, ii, pp. 5-6.

16. Borenius, *Field-Marshal Mannerheim*, p. 30.

17. Carl Enckell, *Politiska minnen*, II, Stockholm, 1956, p. 407.

18. Antti Inkinen, 'Vaihe Mannerheimin nuoruusvuosilta', *Uusi Suomi*, Helsinki, 21.vii.1962, p. 6. This article cites and discusses the family's correspondence with the Secretariat of State.

19. A. A. Ignat'yev, *A Subaltern in Old Russia*, London, 1944, p. 49. Inkinen, 'Vaihe Mannerheimin nuoruusvuosilta', p. 6. The titles of civil servants were equated with officers' ranks according to a table of ranks introduced by Peter the Great.

20. SA. M. 275. *Kadetternas straff journal, 1880-1885*. M. 276. *Protokoll bok.* The resignation did not, however, take effect until 1 July. *Finska Kadettkåren, 1812-1887*, Fredrikshamn, 1890, Bihang 1, p. 45.

21. Nordenskiöld married Anna Maria Mannerheim, Count Carl Robert's youngest sister.

22. He obtained 27 marks, a high 'cum laude'. The gradings were as follows: approbatur, 13-20 marks, cum laude, 21-28, laudatur, 29 or more. Harald Dahlström, 'I Helsingfors lyceum', *Marskalken av Finland friherre Gustaf Mannerheim; krigaren, statsmannen, människan*, Helsingfors, 1953, p. 74.

23. Dahlström, 'I Helsingfors lyceum', p. 72.

24. Mannerheim, *Memoirs*, p. 5. References are normally made to the English translation except where the Swedish original has been abridged.

25. Mannerheim's time at the Corps of Cadets was never mentioned in the Russian army lists, which noted that he was educated at a lyceum in Helsinki and at the Niko-layevskoye Cavalry School. *Cf. Spisok polkovnikam*, S.-Peterburg, 1907.

26. Jägerskiöld, *Den unge Mannerheim*, p. 104.

CHAPTER II

EARLY YEARS IN RUSSIA

St. Petersburg immediately impressed Mannerheim with the greatness of the country whose ruler he had come to serve. From the very first his aims there were high. As already stated, Count Archibald Douglas characterised Mannerheim as 'a man of honour without ambition'.[1] Honour always mattered greatly to him, and he was quick to condemn dishonourable or unchivalrous conduct, but he was not without ambition, especially during his years in Russia. Promotion and success were vitally important to him, partly because he felt the need to rise to the challenge of service in Russia by distinguishing himself, partly because he applied to his own achievement standards even more exacting than he ever applied to the performance of his subordinates. The critical attitude of his family towards his decision to serve in Russia must have intensified these feelings. Failure, which would involve a humiliating return to Finland and financial disaster, was unthinkable. He was aided in the pursuit of his ambitions by his ability, appearance and background, as well as by a capacity for shrewd calculation, though he was not merely an able and resolute climber: his family and friends knew him as a kindly and genial man. But he was also optimistic and self-confident, never doubting his capacity to undertake the responsibilities of command or to implement his plans. In his character can be seen the egotism, the pride, and the determined will of the leader. Circumstances had taught him the value of determination, and determination to overcome whatever obstacles he might encounter in his quest for distinction was perhaps the strongest feature in his character.

On 14 September, 1887 Mannerheim began the two-year course as a *junker*, or officer cadet, at the Nikolayevskoye Cavalry School, a proud establishment founded in 1823, and destined to become known throughout the cavalry as 'The Glorious School', or simply as 'The School'. In his *Memoirs* he recorded that, 'with its greater resources and opportunities for practical work, the training was undoubtedly more rational and efficient than that of the Finnish Corps of Cadets'.[2] The disadvantages of its situation in the city were overcome by a summer camp and frequent participation in the manoeuvres of the St. Petersburg garrison. Mannerheim was at once in his element. He enjoyed the military training, especially appreciating the opportunities to develop and improve his horsemanship, and quickly acquired the cavalryman's easy air of superiority towards civilians and other branches of the service. Horses had become his devoted interest, and being thorough in everything he did, even as a young man, he eagerly learned all he could about them. He rode well and achieved the honour of becoming the first in his class to be allowed the privilege of wearing spurs. Perhaps it was fortunate he became so absorbed in his work, because the occasions when he could go home on leave to Finland were few, and there was little free time in which to get to know St. Petersburg. However, he was not completely isolated from life in the city, since he became acquainted with several Finns who lived there and was entertained by them from time to time.

The place an officer cadet obtained in the passing-out list was of considerable importance. The majority went into the cavalry of the line or the cossacks, but the best could be considered for commissions in the guards' cavalry, or could join another regiment with the benefit of a year's seniority.[3] Prompted by the attractive career opportunities and the delights of the capital, both social and intellectual – since he was alert and keen to improve his mind – Mannerheim wanted a commission in the Chevalier Guards, the premier guards' cavalry regiment, in which some of the most aristocratic Russian families had strong traditions of service. He worked hard to this end and did well at the school, despite another bout of typhoid fever and a gastric illness, both of which necessitated convalescence in Finland and the loss of precious time. Use of a foreign language also posed problems, 'all the more as the speech of many of the teachers was difficult to grasp and their words never seemed to come beyond their bushy Russian beards'.[4] He never lost his accent and his Russian, though adequate, was never perfect. S. de Witt, who became an aide-de-camp to Mannerheim in 1916, remarked on his 'terrible Swedish accent' and added that 'his vocabulary was often deficient'.[5]

Shortage of money was a problem, as always. Uncle Albert was paying his fees, but expenses were greater than they had anticipated, although the Minister-Secretary of State was able to arrange a grant from imperial funds on General Bilderling's recommendation. The size of a man's private income was important when choosing a regiment, and Mannerheim had no money at all. The Chevalier Guards was extremely expensive but would be a good stepping-stone to the General Staff Academy, where he was confident he would be able to live on his pay. Uncle Albert reluctantly agreed to help him raise the money, though he was far from convinced of the wisdom of his nephew's plans. Eventually a loan was arranged from the money to be left to the Mannerheim children by their grandmother Louise von Julin.[6] Meanwhile he continued to strive for a vacancy in the Chevalier Guards.

Vacancies were filled in a complicated way by the War Minister, and sometimes even by the Empress, who was Colonel-in-Chief of the regiment. The serving officers, too, had an important say in the matter since they had the power to reject applicants they considered unsuitable. Mannerheim was helped over this obstacle not only by his ability and prowess as a horseman but by his appearance and background. His appearance gave him great advantages which he used to the full throughout life. He was tall – about 6 feet 4 inches – erect, well-proportioned and handsome. Admiral Sir Walter Cowan, who saw him in 1919, wrote: 'He was, I think, the handsomest foreigner I have ever met. Very tall, gracefully built, and beautifully-made clothes.'[7] His presence commanded immediate attention and respect; it was impossible not to notice him. As a young officer, he acquired the appropriate nickname of 'the knight'. He was well cast for the parts he played in the ceremonial surrounding the Russian court, and it is unlikely that he would have entered the Chevalier Guards if his appearance had been unfavourable, any more than if his background had not been right. Although a foreigner, he was a baron and his father a count. Mannerheim was an important name in Finland. Members of his family had held very high posts in the Finnish administration, and this fact would not be unknown in St. Petersburg, where he had also established valuable connections. But in any case Finns of his class were accepted quite normally in Russian guards' regiments. There could be no doubt that he would fit in: he survived the scrutiny and was accepted by the regiment of his choice.

He passed out of the school as second in the group of *junkers* graded first class,[8] a tribute to his ability and determination, but it was one thing to pass the examination and another to join the Chevalier Guards. For some reason – bureaucratic difficulties, as he himself believed, outside interference, or even genuine bad luck – there was no vacancy available, and when he at last found a regiment to take him it was far from what he wanted. He received his first commission on 22 August, 1889, as a Cornet

33

in the 15th Aleksandriyskiy Dragoon Regiment of HIH Grand Duke Nicolas Nikolayevich the elder.[9] Since he had entered a line cavalry regiment, he received the year's seniority to which his first-class grading entitled him: it was no consolation for the disappointment, and he continued to use every opportunity and every source of influence at his disposal to further his ambition to enter the Chevalier Guards. In June he had written to his godmother, Baroness Alfhild Scalon de Coligny, asking her to appeal to the War Minister or the Empress to obtain a vacancy for him. Ultimately, her appeal to the Empress was successful, but in the meantime he had to join the dragoons, who were stationed close to the German frontier at Kalisz, a small town but one of the oldest in Poland.

He reported there in October 1889 and did not care for what he found. It was a typical garrison and life there was monotonous, even to a newcomer, since there was little for him to do outside his duties with the 3rd Squadron.[10] There were, however, some compensations. The regiment was kept at full strength and was well mounted, adding greatly to the interest and value of training. Mannerheim came to like Poland and the Polish people, although he contrasted unfavourably the disorganised state of affairs in Russian Poland with the order prevailing across the frontier in Prussia. Naturally, he was delighted when at last a vacancy was found for him in the Chevalier Guards. He had already been with his new regiment for seven months when his transfer was published on 8 August, 1891.[11]

He belonged to the Chevalier Guards until 1904, serving in St. Petersburg for most of that time. The contrast with the remote garrison he had left could have been scarcely greater. He was caught up at once in the ceremony and tradition characteristic of guards' regiments as well as in the social life of the capital. The time available for training for war was limited appreciably by the number of reviews, parades, official holidays and periods of guard duty in which the regiment was involved. The situation of the barracks in the centre of St. Petersburg limited opportunities for field training and the horses suffered from want of exercise, notably during the winter when the training programme emphasised individual and theoretical instruction. The officers were then busy with tactical problems and study of the cavalry regulations in readiness for the summer, when the regiment moved to Krasnoye Selo for squadron and regimental manoeuvres. Mannerheim looked forward to the large manoeuvres of all arms held at Krasnoye Selo at the end of the training year, in which the Chevalier Guards joined as part of the 1st Brigade of the 1st Guards Cavalry Division.

As always, he took his duties seriously and worked hard and efficiently. His enthusiasm for his profession was quite untypical and attracted immediate attention. Relatively few Russian officers, especially in the guards, regarded the army as a profession. To many of them, service in the army simply offered the most acceptable solution to the problem of finding suitable employment in an agrarian society. Such officers might resign their commissions and retire to the country on succeeding to their family estates; alternatively, they might enter the diplomatic or civil service. They achieved a superficial familiarity with their duties but had no wish to do more. They found the routine of training irksome, took little interest in energetic activities, and became increasingly absorbed in the enervating life of St. Petersburg society. Their example did not induce Mannerheim to change his ways. Although he recognised very clearly that Russia was not a country in which it was possible to rise by work alone, the repeated warnings of his relations that he was a poor boy who must exert himself to make his way in the world had not been without effect.

Count Aleksey Alekseyevich Ignat'yev, who joined the Chevalier Guards, and eventually became a Lieutenant-General in the Red army wrote:

'My immediate chief turned out to be Lieutenant Baron Mannerheim, the future hangman of the Finnish Revolution. A Swede by origin, a Finn by upbringing, this model mercenary looked on the service as a profession and not as an idle way of passing the time. He could do everything in exemplary fashion, and even drank in such a way that he stayed sober. Deep down, certainly, Mannerheim despised our civilians in regimentals, but he contrived to express his attitude in so jovial a fashion that the majority actually took it all as teasing on the part of the "well-meaning but limited" Baron. His attitude toward me also was shrewd, and he constantly demonstrated to me that, beyond mediocre riding, and also, maybe, a bit of gymnastics, everything else was utterly beyond my ken.'[12]

The description is malicious, but perceptive, and a striking testimony to Mannerheim's competence and his professionalism. There was a simple explanation why he was considered 'limited'. A Chevalier Guards Officer told de Witt in Paris years later that in the regiment the young

Mannerheim was thought of as 'mediocre' primarily because of his appalling Russian.

Shortly after joining the 1st Squadron of the Chevalier Guards (Her Majesty's Squadron), he had become responsible for training the young soldiers who had completed their first year of military service. The patience and attention to detail that contributed to his success as a horseman produced good results in training the Russian soldier, who tended to be lazy and happy-go-lucky, but who responded well to his leadership and whom he found docile and easy to handle. Ignat'yev participated in a 'young soldiers' review' which 'was brilliantly handled by Mannerheim, with the result that I, as well as he, received complimentary citation in regimental orders'.[13]

Guard duty inside the Winter Palace formed part of the routine of every junior officer and represented the simplest aspect of ceremonial life in the Chevalier Guards. A coronation, in which the regiment had by tradition a special place, was the most elaborate. The Chevalier Guards went to Moscow in May 1896 for the coronation of Nicolas II, and Mannerheim was chosen to be one of the four officers who lined the steps leading to the thrones during the service, and afterwards accompanied the Emperor in the procession from the cathedral. It was an exhausting occasion but, like all Orthodox services, deeply impressed Mannerheim with its mystery, colour and magnificence, characteristics which contrasted so strongly with the simplicity of the services of the Lutheran Church of Finland to which he belonged.

Although he was attracted to Russia in several ways, for example by the stimulating cosmopolitan life of the capital, the splendour of the Empire's secular and religious ceremonial and, perhaps above all, by the wide opportunities presented by service in the army of a great power, he never relinquished his Finnish nationality and never allowed his connections with Finland to lapse. He identified himself with his new environment in one important respect only. On 2 May, 1892, he married Anastasia Arapova, a daughter of the late General Nicolas Arapov, Chief of Police in Moscow, and a former officer in the Chevalier Guards; her mother had died in 1890. Mannerheim was twenty-five, his bride twenty. The marriage was probably arranged by Baroness Scalon.[14] Since Anastasia was rich, the arrangement had distinct advantages for Mannerheim. Lacking the private income enjoyed by his fellow-officers, he found life in the Chevalier Guards a constant struggle to make ends meet, and he did not like trying to economise; nor was he good at it. Expenses were enormous and the modest pay went nowhere. The loan fund he had arranged was severely strained, and he was forced to borrow money from his family, especially his uncle, Albert von Julin, who contined to take a warm but troublesome interest in him, and from his sister Eva, who helped him at a critical moment. Now he could repay his debts, and make use of new connections to advance his career. There was no longer the same incentive to enter the General Staff Academy and he made no attempt to do so.

The marriage was, of course, perfectly acceptable to the regimental court of honour, which paid particular attention to the officers' choice of brides. Anastasia, too, was presumably content to have acquired a handsome and well-placed husband, especially as her fortune was perhaps more attractive than her looks. She had an estate, Uspenskoye, near Moscow, and another, Aleksandrovka, in Voronezh Government. There was a large house at Uspenskoye which was expensive and difficult to maintain and Mannerheim soon decided to sell the estate. They acquired another property, Apprikken, in Courland, which was eventually sold in 1906 as part of the settlement of Anastasia's affairs. He had approached the stocking and management of Apprikken with considerable enthusiasm, but much to his disappointment found it impossible, as an absentee landowner, to get his plans implemented. Aleksandrovka, though unprofitable, remained in his hands until the revolution. The possession of these new resources enabled him to live in a more impressive style, and he derived much pleasure from being able to entertain his relatives and friends from Finland at his home in St. Petersburg.

It was not unusual for Finns serving in Russia to marry Russian women, nevertheless his family in Finland were anything but enthusiastic about the match, eventually accepting it with resignation. Before long their forebodings seemed to be justified. The couple appear to have been different in temperament and disposition. Mannerheim was to complain that his wife's indolent nature made her completely incapable of any kind of systematic work.[15] His family considered her unbalanced in temperament. Furthermore, the Mannerheims' interests were different. According to Rodzyanko, her fondness for the social round contrasted with his own outdoor pleasures.[16] They were never deeply attached to each other and even their friendship was soon eroded as conflicts between their strong wills increased. Neither can have been prepared to make concessions to the other. Instead, contradiction and defiance poisoned their relationship. Some conflict certainly centred round the future of their two daughters,

Anastasie born in April 1893, and Sophie born in July 1895, whom their father wanted to grow up as capable Finnish women, rather than as Russian society ladies. Difference in religion – Anastasia was Orthodox – was a further source of friction. At first Mannerheim seems to have regarded his wife and children in a concerned and kindly way but ceased to do so when he failed to derive from marriage the combination of womanly affection, understanding and encouragement to which he was capable of responding. He surely sought satisfaction elsewhere and it has been asserted that his conduct towards his wife, both financial and otherwise, was such as to arouse animosity against him in the Chevalier Guards.[17]

In 1901 Baroness Mannerheim went to the Far East as a Red Cross nurse, returning to convalesce after a carriage accident in which she broke her legs. About a year later she took the girls with her to the south of France and never returned. The break between them had become definite by 1904 and Mannerheim made a financial settlement that would prevent his wife and daughters from suffering; his own means were severely reduced in consequence. He could not get a divorce in Russia and the marriage was not brought to a formal end until 1919, when he obtained a divorce in Finland. He met Anastasia in Paris shortly before her death on 31 December, 1936, and a reconciliation took place which pleased and comforted him. Nevertheless, it remains a fair comment that 'Mannerheim's role as husband and father was not one in which he excelled or in which, perhaps, he was greatly interested.'[18]

The shortness of the marriage freed him from the need to reconcile the obligations of family life with his exacting devotion to the demands of the service. From 1904 he could follow those demands unimpeded by family considerations: this was to be important for the development of his career. A happy family man might not have volunteered for service in Manchuria or undertaken a two-year expedition in Central Asia. The failure of his marriage had a political significance too. He was tied to Russia not only by his oath of allegiance to the Emperor and by his career, but also by an indefinable but real emotional sympathy with the society in which he found the opportunity to fulfil his military and social ambitions. Marriage to a Russian might have weakened his bonds with Finland, which he had left willingly and with a light heart, and diminished his consciousness of his Finnish nationality. However, he was not russified by his marriage and in spite of his bonds with Russia contined to regard Finland as his homeland. Although the situation there was uninviting,

Finland was the obvious place for him to go when revolution destroyed the Russia he had served so loyally.[19]

Perhaps his Finnish nationality was the principal cause of the occasional intrigues against him to which his biographer Rodzyanko refers:[20] Russian attacks on the Finnish constitution and Finnish liberties began at the end of the nineteenth century and Finns serving in Russia found themselves in an invidious position. Intrigues were to be expected in circles close to the court, but they were not typical of Mannerheim's reception in Russia. He was in no sense a foreign outcast. There was no Russian nationalism in the heterogeneous officer corps, in which Poles, Baltic Germans, Lithuanians and Finns served alongside Russians on terms of absolute equality of opportunity and reward and in a spirit of irreproachable comradeship.[21] The great house of 'gay and hospitable Petersburg'[22] were open to him and he became well known in the capital, particularly through his sporting interests. Society life attracted him at first and his friends in the Chevalier Guards ensured he was well launched. He considered the season of 1892 even more successful than that of the previous year, but after his marriage had less time and inclination for social life. His work, too, made greater demands on him. He liked gypsy singing and visits to the ballet and the opera, especially from his thirties when he had the money to pay for the expensive seats guards officers were obliged to take. However, his more obvious pleasures were those of a man of action, and, for the most part, those of a country gentleman. He had acquired a liking for these during his boyhood at Louhisaari at the same time, perhaps, as he acquired his robust constitution. His leisure was occupied by such pursuits as shooting, hunting, fencing, and above all, riding, including show jumping and polo. He was also a frequent prize-winner in the races he entered before Anastasia's fears of an accident led him to give up racing.

His skill with horses prompted in 1897 the offer of a secondment to the Court Stables Unit as assistant to the Director, General von Grünewald, who had commanded the Chevalier Guards before receiving the appointment that year. The importance of the horse – and hence of the Court Stables Unit – can be judged from the fact that the first motor-cars did not arrive in St. Petersburg until 1901 or 1902, and another four or five years passed before the Emperor acquired any.[23] Mannerheim accepted the offer,[24] seeing in it the chance to work constantly with horses and to travel, while at the same time receiving more pay and a higher status. A magnificent apartment adjoining the Imperial Stables and another quarter at Tsarskoye Selo accompanied the post. With these privileges, and his wife's money, he was able to live in a grand manner that was vastly different from the way of life of the Finnish aristocracy. He held various posts in the Court Stables Unit for nearly seven years. The selection of horses for purchase by the Stables, with which he was much concerned, involved interesting visits to England, Germany, Austria-Hungary, France and Belgium. It was fascinating work and permitted him to exercise his good judgment of horses, a quality he had displayed on joining the Chevalier Guards when he bought in Breslau an excellent horse at half the price that a comparable animal would cost in St. Petersburg. Work with horses also involved the risk of accidents. He had a particularly bad one in Berlin in 1898 when one of his knee-caps was smashed by a horse kicking out. For a while there was doubt whether he would be able to return to duty, but after some months in hospital, an operation, and a period of convalescence, he recovered and resumed work.

He had become a Lieutenant in 1893 and a Second Captain in 1899,[25] after waiting well over the usual four-yearly interval between promotions. When he became a Captain in December 1902,[26] he decided it was time to return to the army: he had begun to fear for his career prospects. He was still on the rolls of the Chevalier Guards but was not anxious to return to duty with his regiment, no doubt because there was always a long waiting list for vacancies as squadron commanders. However, in January 1903 he was expecting a squadron command by the autumn, although there was still a possibility that he might instead be posted to the Officers' Cavalry School. But in April he learned that he was to become commander of the School's Model Squadron in June 1903, initially in an acting capacity.[27] His appointment to the permanent staff there came as a pleasant surprise and put an end to his uncertainty about the future. Moreover, it was an especially good job. The commander of the Model Squadron held a privileged position, with a regimental commander's pay, and the chance to go on to command a regiment without an intermediate appointment.

The Officers' Cavalry School in St. Petersburg 'served to give officers both technical and tactical training'.[28] In particular, it prepared selected officers – of whom Mannerheim had believed he might be one – for appointment as squadron commanders, and played a vital part in raising the standard of training and efficiency of the cavalry. The Model Squadron derived its name from its use as a demonstration unit for commanding officers' exercises, and for experiments with new types of equipment.

Mannerheim learned a good deal from General Brusilov, the head of the school, who thought sufficiently highly of his squadron commander to attempt to dissuade him from volunteering to serve in Manchuria on the outbreak of the Russo-Japanese War in 1904 in order to save himself for a likely future European conflict. Mannerheim, however, was not content to continue in the routine of peace-time duties when there was a chance to see active service: as a keen professional officer he regarded training as preparation for battle and was eager to test himself in the field. Here, too, was a golden opportunity to return to regimental service in a senior position which could bring him more quickly to the command of a regiment.

There were also personal reasons behind his decision to volunteer for the front. He was passing through a severe emotional crisis and felt beset by problems that reduced him to despair. The financial difficulties he thought had been solved for good had reappeared when his wife left him, and they may possibly have been increased by misfortune at cards. In any case, the collapse of his marriage had been more than an economic blow. Mannerheim was by no means a calculating careerist devoid of sensibility and feelings of affection. His sister Sophie wrote of his kind, warm nature, which she believed he had inherited from their mother. The character that emerges from his letters is that of a gay, warm-hearted person, as deeply attached to his relatives as they were to him. In their company and that of his friends he found refreshment as well as enjoyment. He was a man to whom the love, understanding and encouragement of women were particularly important. This fact appears clearly from his correspondence during the First World War with Princess Marie Lubomirska, one of his friends in Warsaw, and his letters to her reveal, too, the depth and delicacy of his feelings. Close contact with the formality of the court and high society had, of course, exerted a strong influence on his character, already accustomed to punctilious behaviour as a result of his military training. He had quickly accepted the conventions and etiquette of the capital and had acquired the easy dignity and charm of the cavalier, admiring and admired by attractive women, but now he was weary of society life and badly wanted to get away from St. Petersburg, where the political atmosphere, too, had become uncongenial after the Russian government had initiated its repressive policy in Finland. Towards the end of July, after he had managed to tidy up his financial affairs, he made a formal application for a posting to Manchuria.

On 20 October, 1904, he was transferred to the 52nd Nezhinskiy

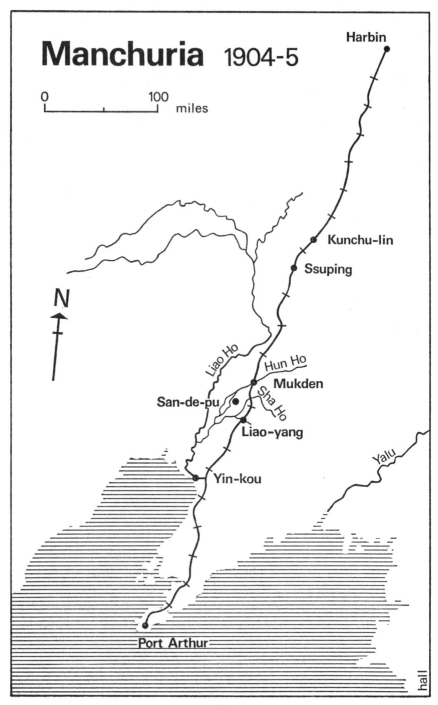

Manchuria 1904-5

0   100
         miles

Harbin

Kunchu-lin

Ssuping

Liao Ho

Hun Ho

Mukden

San-de-pu

Sha Ho

Liao-yang

Yalu

Yin-kou

Port Arthur

N

hall

Manchuria

Dragoon Regiment as a Lieutenant-Colonel for service in the Japanese war.[29] The promotion was automatic on leaving the guards for a line regiment, since officers' ranks in the guards were equivalent to the next higher rank in the rest of the army.[30] He reached Manchuria after a short visit to Vladivostok, the purpose of which he revealed privately to his sister Sophie: he had gone to meet a woman of whom he was fond, who was working in a hospital near there. On 21 November he reported to his regiment, part of the 2nd Independent Cavalry Brigade, which lay in reserve behind the right wing of the Russian army. He was appointed assistant to the regimental commander, and became busy at once trying to counteract the low morale, idleness and drinking prevalent among the officers, a state of affairs that horrified him. Few, however, shared the energy and enthusiasm that led him to volunteer to take part in reconnaissances made by other units behind the Japanese left flank, on one of which he received his baptism of fire.

The general situation had been unfavourable to the Russians from the outset when the Japanese fleet, without a declaration of war, attacked Russian warships at Port Arthur on 8 February, 1904, and caused such losses that Japanese troops were able to move to Korea for the invasion of Manchuria without interference. The attack had been provoked by the expansionist policy pursued by the Russian government in the Far East. Russia had managed to profit from the weakness of China, and prevent Japan from doing the same, to such an extent that the Japanese began to fear for their own security, particularly when in 1903 the Russians delayed giving an assurance that Korea should be regarded as a Japanese sphere of influence.

The Russian army in Manchuria was forced to defend the line of the railway from Harbin to Port Arthur. The country was unprepared for war, and reinforcements and stores had a long, slow journey from Europe along the Trans-Siberian railway. General Kuropatkin, who became supreme commander in the Far East, failed to provide energetic leadership. Morale became low and bad organisation and planning worsened the situation. Not surprisingly, the Japanese retained the initiative. By the middle of May 1904 they had defeated Kuropatkin in the battle of Liao-yang and compelled him to retreat to the Sha-ho.

The first important operation in which Mannerheim participated was the cavalry raid led by General Mishchenko against the port of Yin-kou in January 1905. Kuropatkin's original intention was for the cavalry to cut the railway between Port Arthur and Liao-yang, but he altered this

43

plan, subordinating the attack on the railway to the capture of Yin-kou. The change in the aim of the raid was unfortunate in that its strategic value was greatly diminished. There remained, however, considerable opportunity for a daring commander to disrupt the area behind the Japanese left wing. Mishchenko organised his raiding force of over 7,000 cavalry supported by horse artillery into four columns; Mannerheim was with the Nezhinskiy Dragoons on the right. The raid began on 9 January, 1905. Progress was retarded by the pack animals of the supply train, and instead of pressing on rapidly towards Yin-kou on 10 and 11 January, Mishchenko allowed himself to be held up by detachments of Japanese in the fortified villages. Mannerheim offered to command one of the parties sent out on 11 January to attack the railway, but was told he was too high in rank. No permanent damage was done to the line, and the vital bridges remained unharmed. On 12 January Mishchenko decided to make a night attack on the eastern station at Yin-kou. The Nezhinskiy Dragoons formed part of the reserve and Mannerheim commanded two squadrons covering the right of the Russian artillery.[31] The relatively small attacking force met with prepared resistance, its units became mixed up in the darkness, and the assault failed with heavy losses. Mishchenko then heard that his line of retreat had been cut, and began to retire on 13 January; three days later the raid was over. It had achieved nothing, largely because of its commander's want of speed and daring.

Russian unwillingness to take risks to achieve a worthwhile objective showed itself again in the battle of San-de-pu, which lasted from 25 to 30 January. Mannerheim was engaged in this action, in which the Russian Second Army under General Gripenberg began a cautious but not unsuccessful offensive against the Japanese left. Kuropatkin, however, was unwilling to be drawn into a major operation. The battle of San-de-pu petered out and was followed by a short period of inaction during which the Japanese brought up the army that had just forced Port Arthur to surrender. They resumed the offensive in mid-February 1905. In the ensuing battle of Mukden which lasted until the middle of March, they outflanked and severely defeated the Russian right, forcing the Russian army to withdraw a hundred miles to the north. As a result of the defeat Kuropatkin was replaced as commander-in-chief by General Linevich.

Mannerheim was involved in a great deal of reconnaissance work during the early stages of the battle of Mukden, when the Russians were trying to discover the Japanese dispositions. On one patrol he had his horse shot under him. The Russian official history of the war describes

one unspectacular but fairly typical cavalry task in which he took part at
this time, and which was also reported in the Helsinki newspaper *Hufvudstadsbladet*. On 4 March, when the Japanese were working round the
Russian right flank, he was commanding two detached squadrons of the
Nezhinskiy Dragoons, part of a force operating in conjunction with the
1st Siberian Army Corps under Lieutenant-General Gerngross. Mannerheim was ordered to determine the strength of an enemy column, without
becoming involved in serious fighting. Noticing that a village was occupied by the enemy, he ordered his men to dismount to occupy a neigh-
bouring village. A Japanese force of one and a half to two squadrons,
which had been at first mistaken for Cossacks, suddenly opened up a
fierce fire on them from behind the place as they approached. Seeing no
more enemy beyond the village, and remembering his orders to avoid
battle, he decided to withdraw. His casualties were one killed and ten
wounded.[32] This may have been the action for which he was promoted
to Colonel for bravery on the battlefield.[33] His courage under fire was
generally acknowledged in Manchuria, and one of his fellow-officers was
moved to ask: 'What is the matter with Mannerheim? It seems as if he is
trying to get killed.'[34] This fearless bravery was to be revealed again many
times during and after the First World War and there can be no doubt that
he found the atmosphere of battle exhilarating.

After the battle of Mukden he began to suffer from a severe inflammation
of the left ear. In addition, he had a high temperature and a knee injury.
To avoid delay in obtaining treatment, he travelled north to Kunchu-lin
in a goods wagon of an improvised ambulance train. He was welcomed
there by Professor Richard Faltin, an old school-fellow, who was head of
a Finnish Red Cross ambulance. Mannerheim stayed at their medical
centre a fortnight, visiting daily an ear specialist at a nearby ambulance
from Riga. But nothing could be done to save the hearing of his left ear.
Despite this, he was soon back in action, taking part in some reconnaissances with his regiment. Later in 1905 he led a force of Chinese native
cavalry in a raid far behind the Japanese left flank.

There were no major land operations after the battle of Mukden. In
May the Russians suffered disaster at sea when their Baltic Fleet, which
had sailed round to the Pacific, was annihilated at the battle of Tsushima.
Both sides were now ready for peace, Japan because its resources in men
and money were nearing exhaustion, Russia because of internal discontent and increasing war-weariness. An offer by the President of the United
States to act as mediator was rapidly accepted. The peace treaty was

1905 signed at Portsmouth, New Hampshire, on 5 September, 1905. The Russian lease of the Liao-tung peninsula with Port Arthur was ceded to Japan. Korea became a Japanese protectorate and Russia had to evacuate Manchuria. Discontent in Russia was exacerbated by defeat and finally broke into revolution. The Emperor had wavered between a policy of repression and one of concession: the general strike of October 1905 led to concessions. A manifesto was issued granting a liberal constitution. Nevertheless, armed risings took place all over Russia during the last months of 1905 and some army units mutinied. For a time the state appeared in danger of collapse, but as the public calmed down the government adopted a firm policy and used the guards and other loyal troops – notably cavalry – to restore order. Mannerheim explained the loyalty of the cavalry with the comment that 'care of his horse took up so much of the cavalryman's time that he had little opportunity for politics and conspiracy'.[35]

Units were returning to their peace establishments at the end of 1905 and Mannerheim was no longer required for active duty with the Nezhinskiy Dragoons. He preferred to get himself ordered back to St. Petersburg on sick leave in November 1905 instead of staying in the Far East until the regiment was withdrawn. The war had not taught him so much as he had hoped, though he felt he had tested his capacity to some extent. In letters home he had criticised the under-employment of the cavalry, which he felt might have been avoided had there been more talented cavalry generals among the commanders. He had certainly realised the deficiencies of the Russian army and learned, too, some of the limitations of the cavalry arm. The special honour of a battlefield promotion to Colonel, which he was promised in April and for which he waited anxiously until December, marked an important step in his career. To reach the rank of Colonel at the age of thirty-eight was creditable, though not in itself exceptional, but in Mannerheim's case it marked a very rapid advance. When he left for the front, he had only been a squadron commander for just over a year; on his return he was on the list of those awaiting the command of a regiment. He had enhanced his peace-time reputation as a capable officer and had shown that he could lead men bravely in battle.

The army in Manchuria had not been much affected by the revolution in Russia, but he had run into the disorders on the way home. Chaos prevailed all along the Trans-Siberian railway as mutinous soldiers disrupted traffic. The journey to the capital took him thirty-one days and he did not arrive there until the beginning of January 1906. He was then sent on long leave because of the state of his health: the rigorous conditions of Manchuria had brought on rheumatism, a complaint from which he was to suffer considerably in the future. Returning to Europe meant he would again have to face his family and financial problems. However, his vitality had reasserted itself in the atmosphere of war and he had overcome the mood of depression in which he had left for the front. The prospect of leave was welcome and it was with great pleasure that he left St. Petersburg for Finland.

The harmonious relationship that had existed between Finland and Russia at the time Mannerheim joined the imperial army had come to an end before the turn of the century. Russian nationalists had long resented the status of Finland as an autonomous constitutional monarchy and viewed with misgivings the growth of Finnish nationalism with its emphasis on the legal distinction between the Grand Duchy of Finland and the rest of the Empire. After the accession of Nicolas II, Finland lost the protection previously afforded by the goodwill of the sovereign, and the nationalists became predominant in the Russian government and began to attack Finnish liberties and institutions.[36] The attack was not only ideological: the Russian military authorities were gravely concerned about the inadequacy of Finland's defences. In 1898 the Russian War Ministry proposed a law which threatened the Finnish army with the loss of its separate identity. The opposition of the Finnish Diet to this Army Law was overcome by the imperial manifesto of February 1899 which virtually put an end to the Diet's legislative functions. In 1901 the Finnish army was dissolved and Finns were required to serve in the Russian army; the Corps of Cadets was closed. Civil servants who refused to carry out illegal orders were dismissed.

Finns who concerned themselves with political developments reacted to these measures in two ways, and although the protagonists of each approach had the same aim – the re-establishment of lawful conditions in Finland – the split between them became deep and bitter. The 'constitutionalists' saw the conflict in moral terms. It was a matter of principle to them that the law had to be obeyed, and therefore the ruler who issued illegal decrees had to be disobeyed. The so-called 'compliants' considered the conflict in political terms and sought to solve the crisis by coming to an agreement with the Russians. They were prepared to co-operate with the Russians to prevent the development of a complete impasse in Finno-Russian relations, and to keep open a means of restoring contact between

47

the Emperor and the Finnish people when conditions improved. Gradually the Swedish and Young Finn parties took the 'constitutionalist' line, and the Old Finns that of the 'compliants'. Constitutionalist opposition took the form of a highly organised passive resistance movement concerned above all with the prevention of the operation of the conscription law. One of its leaders was Mannerheim's brother Carl. The Russians were infuriated and intensified the repression, expelling Carl Mannerheim and several others from the country in 1903. The following year, General Bobrikov, the detested Governor-General of Finland, was assassinated. Demands for active resistance were growing when the Russian revolution of 1905 began. The 'constitutionalists' had followed developments in Russia and used this opportune moment to exert pressure on the authorities. The Finnish Social Democrat party organised a general strike, and, as in Russia, the Emperor capitulated. The repressive decrees were withdrawn and a new ministry was formed from members of the 'constitutionalist' parties which had supported the passive resistance movement.

Russian oppression in Finland, and its consequences for his family, made Mannerheim's own position as a Finnish officer in the Russian army extremely delicate. In his *Memoirs* he affirmed his opposition to the russification of Finland,[37] and his actions at the time revealed his concern about the course of events. For example, he came to Helsinki to confer with his family when he heard about Carl's expulsion, and he helped the Finnish constitutionalists with information about events in St. Petersburg and with advice on how to contact persons in Russia who were sympathetic towards Finland. His own closest social connections in the capital were with the more liberal elements of Russian society, who favoured the introduction of constitutional monarchy, for example the salon of Countess Betsy Shuvalova but others there regarded unfavourably his association with people in Finland who were bitterly opposed to Russian policy. While in Helsinki in May 1903 he learned of a rumour that he would be forced to leave the service because of what was called the Finnish agitation. It came as an unpleasant shock and for a time he had considered resigning his commission: his family dissuaded him at that stage. Resignation became inconceivable after the outbreak of war in 1904, since he felt it would have been disloyal to the army to resign during a time of national crisis. A man who wanted to serve in the Russian army and achieve distinction in its ranks, in spite of his experience of personal injustice, could no longer have doubts about volunteering for service in Manchuria when Russian arms were suffering defeat after defeat.[38] It was only natural that he should feel personally involved when part of the army to which he belonged came into action, and from that moment political considerations were subordinated to feelings of loyalty and obligation to the Empire and sympathy for the army, and to a practical, almost instinctive, professional desire to take part in the campaign.

He was, in fact, in danger of incurring suspicion both in Russia and Finland. Already during the early 1890s his family, who were sensitive to signs of a deteriorating atmosphere of Finno-Russian relations, had begun to fear the environment of St. Petersburg was making him develop a Russian outlook, and his decision to volunteer for service in Manchuria came as a great blow to them. His relations, especially Carl, though sympathetic to his predicament, could not see how a patriotic Finn could possibly justify such an action on the grounds Mannerheim put forward, namely that he was fighting for the country and not its government, and that to do so would further his career and help to solve his personal problems. To continue to serve in the imperial army was now bad enough; to volunteer to fight for the Emperor-oppressor was virtually incomprehensible – patriotic Finns even disliked their countrymen serving in Red Cross ambulances in Manchuria – but in the end Mannerheim's family resigned themselves to his arguments. It has been suggested that he volunteered to fight in Manchuria as a deliberate demonstration of his loyalty to his new country and to the Emperor,[39] but the disturbed state of his feelings in 1904 makes it difficult to single out any one motive in this way. Moreover, his reaction to Russian oppression in Finland had been, from the outset, conditioned above all by the circumstances prevailing throughout the earlier, and greater, part of his service in Russia, when loyalty to the Emperor had been absolutely compatible with loyalty to Finland. This habitual loyalty, his emotional ties with both Finland and Russia, and his strong career interest in the Empire, were sufficient to lead him to hope for a change in Russian policy that would resolve the difficulties experienced since 1899 by Finns serving in the Empire. It is not, therefore, surprising that he soldiered on in the expectation of that change in policy, although doing so laid him open to the charge that he was putting Emperor, army, career and self before national and family considerations.

The respect for constitutional legality and political liberty that pervaded the thought of his family and friends – as of Finns in general who were concerned with politics – communicated itself to him before he left

Finland, becoming and remaining an important part of his own political outlook. The autocracy in Russia, with its potentially powerful but often inefficient bureaucracy, the stifling of personal initiative and ensuing indecision, evidence of which he had seen in plenty in the high command in Manchuria, did not appeal to him. He was to comment on the value of initiative, responsibility, enterprise, and freedom from oppression when investigating conditions in China in 1906–08. Years later, he was to stress the importance of individual responsibility based on a sense of justice.[40] He believed in law and order, and the belief in law was strong; only in the exceptional circumstances of July 1919 was he tempted to put political expediency before the spirit of constitutional legality, and he resisted that temptation. With this outlook, it was impossible for him to regard russification measures – in Finland and elsewhere – with anything other than abhorrence.

Living in a Russian environment had, however, exerted a considerable influence on his views. Experience of the Russian government in action, together with regular contact with the various shades of political and social opinion in St. Petersburg, had sharpened his political awareness and matured his judgment both of policies and people. This experience, one of the most significant and enduring consequences of his service in Russia, was naturally reflected in his attitude to Finnish affairs, though not in the sense that he approved of either the aims or the methods of the Slavo-philes. However, separation from the emotional atmosphere of opposition in which his family lived enabled him to see the situation more dispas-sionately and in clearer perspective. They saw with despair a sustained and apparently widely supported Russian offensive against Finland. He knew from his contacts in the capital that the Russian policy of oppression was not supported unanimously by the educated classes, nor even by the whole of the imperial family. 'La Russie libérale, radicale et socialiste se mit, comme un seul homme, du côté des finlandais.'[41] Some Russians recognised that an oppressive policy was not dictated by Russian state needs. V. I. Gurko, who was at this time an official in the Imperial Chancellery, afterwards wrote: 'Russia's only interest in Finland was in being absolute master of the Finnish Gulf and the Finnish coast and in having an absolutely secure frontier line between Russia and Finland in view of its proximity to St. Petersburg.'[42] Mannerheim realised this, too, and his understanding of Russian concern for the security of St. Petersburg was always reflected in his policy towards Russia.

Mannerheim also perceived the growth of tensions within Russia that would sooner rather than later compel the government to liberalise its approach. The oppression of Finland, though unpleasant, was only a passing phase in Russian policy that would be brought to an end when the elements in the Empire opposed to the extreme nationalists and the autocracy asserted themselves. An alternative solution to the crisis was the negotiation of a political settlement with the existing Russian authorities. Mannerheim was critical of the intransigent attitude and pronouncements of some of the Finnish constitutionalists, which merely exacerbated relations with the Empire, and by offending the susceptibilities of Russia as a great power diminished the chance of reaching an agreement. Such a settlement was all the more desirable since Finland was bound to Russia by its geographical position as well as by their common sovereign. This line of thought on Finno-Russian relations did not reflect the rigid moral viewpoint of the constitutionalists, and bore more resemblance to the approach of the 'compliants'. Yrjö-Koskinen, the leader of the Old Finns, put forward a similar argument, claiming that history had placed Finland in such a position in relation to the Russian Empire that its existence as a nation depended on living in friendship and harmony with the Russians. Provocation, which could only alienate the Russian nation and sovereign, was not, therefore, a sensible policy for the Finns to pursue.

Mannerheim's attitude was thus more pragmatic than that of the 'constitutionalists', and he had little of their confidence in the inevitability of the ultimate triumph of Finland's just cause. However, his optimistic belief in the likelihood of constitutional change in Russia was shared by many constitutionalists, above all by Leo Mechelin – an old friend of the Mannerheim family – and was an argument much used against the Old Finns' readiness to make concessions to the existing Russian government. Like his family, Mannerheim wanted to see an end to the Russian oppression of Finland, but his approach to Finnish–Russian relations differed considerably from theirs, and especially from the extreme constitutionalist position of Carl. He did not make the characteristic gesture of the 'constitutionalist' opposition and resign his commission. An attitude in some respects bordering on compliance, perhaps founded initially on habit and reinforced by inertia, but capable of rational justification, fitted in very well with his ambition to make a successful career in Russia. Nevertheless, the revolution of 1905 appeared to confirm his appreciation of the situation and justify his attitude.

Mannerheim, who was sympathetic towards the Russian constitutionalists, and convinced of the danger of opposing the reforms he believed necessary to pacify society in the Empire, was heartened by the October manifesto. He was relieved at the restoration of legality in Finland, but the process of revolution there was far from his liking. He was horrified to read of the Governor-General of Finland parleying with the revolutionaries, and was not alone in his alarm at the appearance of the Red Guards in Helsinki as a new factor in politics and as a threat to society. Nevertheless, it seemed as if the constitutional troubles of Finland were over after the revolution.

The Diet had assembled in December 1905 to discuss representational reform. It was the last meeting of the four Estates of Nobles, Clergy, Burgesses and Peasants. From February to June 1906 Mannerheim sat in the Estate of Nobles as head of the baronial branch of his family, although he did not speak in the debates.[43] There was general agreement on the need for reform, but cumbersome procedure and hesitation over the magnitude of the proposed changes delayed progress. The reform bill provided for a unicameral legislature of two hundred members elected by universal suffrage, a change Mannerheim regarded as 'absurd' at a time of general ferment.[44] His cautious approach to parliamentary reform was by no means unique among the Swedish-speaking liberal constitutionalists with whom he associated in the Estate of Nobles. An amendment in favour of a two-chamber system was put forward in the Estate of Nobles but was heavily defeated, largely because of a reluctance to take responsibility for the consequences which would have ensued from a rejection of the government's proposal.[45] Acceptance of the bill, Mannerheim felt, was an act of great generosity on the part of the Estates:[46] the Social Democrats thought otherwise. The Emperor gave his assent to the reform bill in July, and the Diet rose in September 1906. Events appeared to justify the hopeful opinions Mannerheim had encountered on his return to Finland earlier that year, but with characteristic foresight he recognised the potential danger of the situation. The independent tone Finnish politicians adopted in dealing with Russia was unlikely to win sympathy for Finland in St. Petersburg, and the difference in character between the conservatism of the Russian government and the liberalism and socialism represented in the democratic Finnish parliament could lead to serious difficulties.

REFERENCES

1. Archibald Douglas, 'Mannerheim', *Svensk tidskrift*, 38, Uppsala, 1951, p. 76.
2. Mannerheim, *Memoirs*, p. 6.

3. E. Bujac, *L'Armée russe: son histoire, son organisation actuelle*, Paris, 1894, pp. 90–1.

4. Mannerheim, *Minnen*, i, p. 19.

5. Mannerheim's French was better than his Russian, though Kalle Lehmus stated that his best languages were undeniably Swedish and Russian. The story Lehmus told to illustrate Mannerheim's knowledge of Russian invites cautious treatment. In the autumn of 1945 he asked a member of the Soviet Control Commission in Helsinki his opinion of Mannerheim's Russian. 'The unreserved reply was that "comparatively few Soviet citizens of the present generation are able to employ in everyday use of the language such beautifully formed and richly illustrated Russian as Mannerheim. His use of the Russian language brings unintentionally to mind such classic authors as Gogol, Turgenev, Pushkin and Dostoyevsky." ' Lehmus, *Tuntematon Mannerheim*, p. 237.

6. Lovisa (known as Louise) was in fact stepmother and aunt to Hélène Mannerheim. She was the sister of Hélène's mother Charlotta von Julin, née Jägerskiöld.

7. Quoted by Lionel Dawson, *Sound of the Guns; being an account of the Wars and Service of Admiral Sir Walter Cowan*, Oxford, 1949, p. 155.

8. Shkot, *Istoricheskiy ocherk Nikolayevskago kavaleriyskago uchilishcha, byvshey Shkoly gvardeyskikh podpraporshchikov i kavaleriyskikh yunkerov. 1823–1898*, S.-Peterburg, 1898, p. 68.

9. *Ego Imperatorskoye Velichestvo . . . prikaz*, 10/22 August, 1889. This series is cited as *Prikaz*.

10. 3rd Squadron according to a contemporary letter quoted by Jägerskiöld, *Den unge Mannerheim*, p. 143. 2nd Squadron according to Mannerheim, *Memoirs*, p. 7. He may, of course, have served in both, but the memoirs are inaccurate on several points from these early years in Russia: e.g. his promotion to Captain is dated two years too soon.

11. *Prikaz*, 27 July/8 August, 1891. On transferring to the guards Mannerheim lost a year in seniority. He was transferred on probation to the Chevalier Guards on 1/13 December, 1890, *Posluzknoy spisok*.

12. Ignat'yev, *A Subaltern in Old Russia*, p. 74. De Witt remarked that Mannerheim 'normally liked to drink a lot. He kept sober, but did not refuse toasts.'

13. Ignat'yev, *A Subaltern in Old Russia*, p. 74.

14. Jägerskiöld, *Den unge Mannerheim*, pp. 187–8.

15. Letter to Sophie Mannerheim, 23.iv.1915, quoted by Jägerskiöld, *Den unge Mannerheim*, p. 203.

16. Rodzyanko, *Mannerheim*, pp. 50–2.

17. *Christian Swanljungs Anmärkningar . . . till marskalk Mannerheims memoirer*. Mannerheim Museum.

18. Warner, *Marshal Mannerheim and the Finns*, p. 31.

19. His return to Finland did not, of course, in itself imply attachment to the country: many Russians fled to Finland, where they were conveniently placed to observe events in Petrograd.

20. Rodzyanko, *Mannerheim*, p. 68. Donner mentioned that Mannerheim experienced personal injustice during the years of oppression in Finland. Donner, *Sotamarsalkka vapaaherra Mannerheim*, p. 19.

21. Carl Enckell, *Politiska minnen*, I, Stockholm, 1956, pp. 14–15.

22. Mannerheim, *Memoirs*, p. 9.

23. A. A. Mosolov, *At the Court of the last Tsar*, London, 1935, pp. 249-51. The Court Stables Unit (Pridvornaya Konyushennaya Chast) was one of the Special Establishments of the Ministry of the Imperial Court.

24. His attachment was published in *Prikaz*, 2/14 September, 1897.

25. Lieutenant, 11 September, 1893; Second Captain, 3 August, 1899. *Prikaz*, 30 August/11 September, 1893. *Prikaz po voyskam gvardii i Peterburgskago Voyennago Okruga*, No. 36, 5/17 August, 1899. This series is cited as *Prikaz po voyskam gvardii*. On conditions governing promotions at this time see Bujac, *L'Armée russe*, pp. 99-100.

26. *Prikaz po voyskam gvardii*, No. 61, 16/29 December, 1902.

27. Mannerheim never held a permanent squadron command in the Chevalier Guards. He commanded the regimental baggage train at one time. His attachment to the Officers' Cavalry School was dated 11 June, 1903, and his appointment to the permanent staff 13 September, 1904. *Posluzhnoy spisok*.

28. Mannerheim, *Memoirs*, p. 13.

29. *Prikaz po voyskam gvardii*, No. 49, 18/31 October, 1904.

30. *Die russische Armee in Krieg und Frieden*, Berlin, 1890, p. 11. The rank of major did not exist at this time.

31. *Guerre russo-japonaise, 1904-1905: histoire rédigé à l'État-major général de l'armée russe*, IV, 2, *Raid d'Yingkeou*, Paris, 1912, p. 76.

32. *Guerre russo-japonaise, 1904-1905*, V, 1, *Bataille de Moukden*. Paris, 1913, pp. 399-400. *Hufvudstadsbladet*, Helsingfors, 10.iii.1905.

33. The account in the official history is similar to that in Mannerheim, *Memoirs*, pp. 20-1. The promotion to Colonel was published in *Prikaz*, 28 November/11 December, 1905. The seniority was dated from 19 February/4 March, *Posluzhnoy spisok*.

34. Hugo Backmansson, 'Spridda hågkomster', *Marskalken av Finland friherre Gustaf Mannerheim; krigaren, statsmannen, människan*, Helsingfors, 1953, p. 80.

35. Mannerheim, *Memoirs*, p. 22.

36. Finland was not the only object of attack. At the end of the nineteenth century the Baltic provinces lost much of their administrative autonomy and German its position as an official language there. However, even after the implementation of measures of russification in Finland, the degree of freedom enjoyed by its population remained higher than in the rest of the empire.

37. Mannerheim, *Memoirs*, p. 76.

38. Donner, *Sotamarsalkka vapaaherra Mannerheim*, p. 19.

39. Nopanen, *Carl Gustaf Emil Mannerheim*, p. 18.

40. Borenius, *Field-Marshal Mannerheim*, pp. 248-9.

41. Conférence politique russe, *Mémoire sur la question finlandaise*, Paris, 1919, pp. 9-10.

42. V. I. Gurko, *Features and Figures of the Past: Government and Opinion in the Reign of Nicholas II*, Stanford, 1939, p. 50.

43. He was present from 10 February to 31 May and 12-26 June, 1906. *Protokoll förda hos Finlands Ridderskap och Adel vid Landtdagen år 1905-06*, Helsingfors, 1906-07, 2 vols. The index (ii, p. 973) shows that he did not speak.

44. Jägerskiöld, *Gustaf Mannerheim*, p. 139.

45. Jussi Teljo, *Suomen valtioelämän murros, 1905-1908*, Porvoo, 1949, p. 66.

46. Mannerheim, *Memoirs*, p. 24.

I.   Mannerheim as a Captain at the Officers' Cavalry School in 1904.

II. Mannerheim as a Major-General in 1914, wearing the parade uniform of His Majesty's Life Guard Uhlan Regiment.

CHAPTER III

ACROSS ASIA

Tento in Mongolia

& see Curzon (??. Egerton) 1906

Mannerheim expected his leave in Finland to last until the middle of
April 1906 and believed he would soon be back from a visit to St. Petersburg in March. However, he was summoned to report to the Chief of the
General Staff, General Palitsyn, and asked if he was willing to take part
in an archaeological expedition led by the French Professor Paul Pelliot
through the border provinces of China from Turkestan to Peking. His
task would be to collect military and political intelligence. The expedition,
due to start in the summer, was expected to take two years. The proposi-
tion came as a complete surprise.[1]

The General Staff's interest in China stemmed from the expansionist
policy Russia had pursued in Asia for several decades, first in Turkestan
and later also in Manchuria. The Russians were not prepared to risk a
conflict with a great power by advancing into what they regarded as
constituted states, but the territories bordering on the Chinese Empire
and nominally subject to it lay open to intervention. Thus by the 1890s
they had absorbed the khanates of Western Turkestan, though their
hopes of permanent territorial gains in Eastern Turkestan had been
frustrated by the reimposition of Chinese colonial rule in the area at the
end of the 1870s with the defeat of the rebellious Dungans – Turkic-
speaking Moslems living on both sides of the Tien Shan – and the recapture
of the oases round the Takla Makan desert that had been seized by a
military adventurer named Yakub Beg. War between Russia and China
was narrowly averted in 1881 when the Chinese tried to force the Russians
to restore Dzungaria, which they had occupied in 1871 during the
Dungan revolt. Russian troops did not evacuate Kuldja, the chief town,
until 1883, and relations between the two powers continued to be strained.

The systematic exploration of Chinese Turkestan – Sinkiang – proceeded
against this political background, with geography, ethnography and
linguistics as the main fields of study. By 1890 the outline of the maps

E   55

had become clearer and the main routes had been frequently used by Europeans. At the turn of the century archaeologists began excavations in the region that were to reveal the existence there of an important Indo-European Buddhist civilisation before the arrival of Islam. British interest in Central Asia underlined the political significance of the work of Russian explorers, whose activity was stimulated by the achievements of Nikolai Mikhailovich Przheval'skiy and facilitated by the establishment of Russian consulates at several places in Sinkiang.

Any increase in the power of the central government in China was likely to have repercussions in all the border territories and be to the disadvantage of China's neighbours. Russian hopes of acquiring parts of Sinkiang and of using the Chinese Eastern Railway to establish their hegemony in Manchuria would be ruined if the weak Chinese government were replaced by a strong administration determined to defend the territorial integrity of the country and able to create the means to do so. The humiliating consequences of the failure of the Boxer rebellion caused the need for a wide range of reforms to be recognised in China, even by the powerful and hitherto reactionary dowager Empress Ts'u-hsi. During the next few years the government began to attempt to strengthen its authority at the expense of the mandarins, create a modern army and educational system, develop communications, especially railways, promote mining and industry, organise welfare in the towns and campaign against opium smoking.

These reforms attracted the attention of the Russians, and since they affected China's military potential, naturally interested the General Staff. In 1901 a decree had ordered the reorganisation of the Chinese military forces, which were hopelessly antiquated in equipment and methods and handicapped by their provincial structure, but little was accomplished. In 1905 another decree provided for the establishment of officers' training schools and the Army Board was reorganised the following year. The lesson of the Russo-Japanese War – that an eastern state using western methods could defeat a European power – was not lost on the Chinese, who began determined efforts to organise a national army. It was evident by 1906 that army reform was making progress.

Neither Mannerheim's personal qualities and recent experience in the Far East, nor the tendency of the General Staff to look on officers who had served in Manchuria as a disturbing element to be got out of the way if possible,[2] seem sufficient in themselves to explain his selection for the mission. It was possibly connected in some way with a plan to ride across

Mongolia which he had devised after the end of the war in Manchuria. The explosive political situation caused him to regret this plan since he did not want to be so far away from the main centres of events at a critical time. He secured sick leave instead and came home, but details of his scheme may have been filed by the authorities and brought to light when an officer was required for the expedition through northern China.[3] Alternatively, someone may simply have remembered his interest in the area. His Finnish nationality was to be turned to good account by the Russian authorities, but there is no evidence to suggest that his selection for the mission was in any way dependent on it.

General Palitsyn's proposal necessitated a difficult decision and he hesitated, tactfully declaring the reason to be his insufficient knowledge of Central Asia and China. He knew he was on the list of officers awaiting the command of a regiment, but could not dismiss lightly an invitation from the Chief of the General Staff, and an unusual opportunity to achieve distinction, even though it imposed for the moment an unwelcome check on the progress of his career and involved a long exile from civilisation. There were, however, compensations, notably the chance to escape from the political pressures likely to accompany the re-establishment of reactionary policies after the concessions of 1905. Nor can the prospect of establishing a reputation as an explorer be dismissed from his thoughts. Przheval'skiy and Kozlov had begun as army officers, and he was conscious, too, of the distinguished example of his uncle, Adolf Erik Nordenskiöld, whose voyage in the *Vega* had so impressed him as a boy. He had already felt the fascination of Asia, and as he studied reports of previous missions in the area his interest grew. Finally his enthusiasm was aroused; he accepted the task and began a few months' intensive preparation.

The objectives of Mannerheim's mission, as approved by the Chief of the General Staff, were listed by him in his report as follows:

'to collect information and military statistics about the region to be covered by the expedition [i.e. the provinces of Sinkiang, Kansu, Shensi, Honan and Shansi], paying particular attention to the provinces of China which lie beyond the Great Wall; to observe the extent to which reforms inaugurated by the Chinese government in recent years had actually been carried out on the spot; to inform myself of the state of the country's defence, and about the reorganisation and training of the troops; to discover the extent to which the provinces traversed had been colonised by the Chinese, and to which the administrative system had been reformed by the Central Government; to discover the mood of the population, its attitude in relation to Chinese policy, the advance of regions and local tribes towards autonomy, and the role played in this connection by the Dalai Lama, popular opinion with regard to Russia and Japan, and the extent to which Japanese influence had noticeably affected measures taken by the Chinese government; to investigate the routes towards Kashgar, and thence onwards to Lanchow and Peking, more especially with a view to discovering the best way in which to move our cavalry detachments and self-contained detachments of all three types of troops towards Lanchow.

'In addition to the foregoing, I had certain special tasks, as follow:

(1) Mapping the route Kashgar – Guldzhat-Davan – Uch-Turfan and along the river Taushkan-Darya.

(2) Exploration of the river Taushkan-Darya from its source in the mountains to where it joins the Yarkend-Darya, as a line of defence.

(3) Compilation of military statistical material about the oasis of Aksu.

(4) Exploration of the route Aksu – Kuldja through the Muzart Pass.

(5) Exploration of the Yulduz Valley.

(6) Discovery of the state of preparedness of the town of Lanchow as a military base.'[4]

The accomplishment of this extensive programme would enable the Russian authorities to form a comprehensive intelligence appreciation of the area, on the basis of which they could prepare plans for war with China, including offensive operations in Sinkiang.

The secret nature of the mission required a cover plan, which was afforded by the association with Pelliot's expedition. This expedition was planned under the auspices of the Académie des Inscriptions et Belles Lettres and the French Ministry of Public Instruction, and of the French Committee of the International Association for the Archaeological, Ethnographic and Linguistic Exploration of Central Asia and the Far East, founded in St. Petersburg as an outcome of the Twelfth International Congress of Orientalists. Its aim was to study the traces and remains, particularly the inscriptions, of the pre-Mohammedan Buddhist period in Sinkiang and north-west China. Its leader, Paul Pelliot, the young and eminent Professor of Chinese at the École française d'Extrême Orient at

Hanoi, had been promised all kinds of privileges on the journey he had planned from Kashgar through Aksu, Kucha, Urumchi, Turfan, Lob Nor, Ansi, Lanchow and Sianfu to Peking.[5] Mannerheim's participation in the expedition was discussed in Paris and St. Petersburg, the final conditions being worked out with Pelliot in the Russian capital. It was agreed that Mannerheim should have complete independence in his work and in matters of equipment and engaging personnel. He was to join Pelliot in Tashkent in May or June.

It was essential not to reveal his identity as a Russian officer. The Russian authorities therefore proposed that he should travel with a French passport, but when the French Ministry of Foreign Affairs refused to give him one they decided instead to let him travel as a Finnish scientist, thus making good use of his nationality. The passport issued to him in Peking was to be sent to Kucha, together with those of other members of Pelliot's expedition. Relations with the Chinese authorities had however, to be established in Kashgar. It was there that he received a pass from a Chinese official made out, with unexpected precision, to the Russian subject, the Finn Baron Mannerheim, whose Chinese name is MA-DA-KHAN'.[6] This name, 'the horse that leaps through the clouds',[7] sounded very fine to the Chinese when they read it on his visiting cards but was also to prove embarrassing. It was usual for foreigners to select Chinese names that sounded more or less recognisable as their own. Mannerheim did not know this, and when, in Kuldja, he had to show the passport obtained from Peking, which gave his name more correctly as Ma-nu-ör-hei-mu, the fact that he was travelling under two names aroused suspicion on the part of the Chinese officials which his explanation did not easily quell. The matter was reported further, and the Governor in Urumchi remarked jokingly that after being called Ma-da-han he had turned up in Kuldja with the name Ma-nu-ör-hei-mu; finally when he reached the Russian embassy in Peking, he was shown a newspaper cutting asking what kind of foreigner it was who had two passports, photographed bridges, mapped roads, measured heights, and generally halted at places of military importance.

To minimise his connections with the Russian Empire, he arranged to receive correspondence from Finland via his relatives in Sweden, and instructed his father to abstract from his letters items of interest to the Chief of General Staff, to whom he referred as Feda, and transmit them to St. Petersburg in a concise form. Although the Chief of the General Staff was known as Feda Palitsyn,[8] this method of referring to him probably afforded adequate security. Mannerheim reported: 'I had orders to conceal the fact that I was an officer, and to travel in the guise of a private Finn, who was a member of various scientific societies. In order to keep myself strictly incognito, I did not reveal my calling even to the Cossacks and made a practice of keeping my diary, my surveys and all my notes in Swedish.'[9] He claimed that nobody in southern Sinkiang took him to be a Russian and that, as far as Kuldja, where the passport problem arose, he was thought to be Swedish. His interpreter, who, like the mandarins, had never heard of Finland, noticed that he had the same religious faith and spoke the same language as the Swedish missionaries, and decided to explain that Sweden and Finland were about the same thing. This deception evidently continued to succeed even for a few months after his nationality had been described precisely on the pass issued to him in Kashgar in January 1907. The success of the cover plan in southern Sinkiang can be judged from the reports of the Indian government's agent in Kashgar. George Macartney, Special Assistant for Chinese Affairs to the Resident in Kashmir, reported the arrival of Pelliot's party in Kashgar 'with a Finn, named Baron Mannerheim, who is to make an archaeological collection for the Helsingfors Museum'. Later he described Mannerheim as a 'Finnish traveller now in Kashgar'.[10] Although the British were getting ample evidence of Russian interest in routes along the Chinese border,[11] they thus remained ignorant of Mannerheim's military work.

From Kuldja onwards there was no concealing from the Chinese his status as a Russian subject and he was no longer accepted as a Swede. At the same time the attitude of the Chinese authorities towards him changed and not to his advantage. The misunderstanding over his passport and his consequent fear of compromising the whole of his expedition made reconnaissance in Ili impossible. From Sianfu onwards the authorities became rather more suspicious, putting difficulties in his way if he attempted to depart in the least from the route broadly outlined in his passport. This specification of the route was a disadvantage compared with a permit for general travel over certain definite provinces. Strong attempts were made at Taiyuan to prevent his journey to the Dalai Lama at Utaishan. He had at all times to act circumspectly and with tact if the outcome of his mission were not to be jeopardised.

It is impossible to say whether the initiative behind the scientific work which formed an integral part of his cover lay with Mannerheim or with the General Staff. In any case, activities which he may have undertaken initially only as cover quickly attained significance in their own right. He wrote in his report – which was not, of course, the place to enlarge on his non-military activities – that he made anthropometric observations and collected ethnographic material 'mainly with the object of making my work look scientific to my fellow-travellers and to the Chinese authorities. . . . I usually switched over to this kind of work after a period of time spent on long journeys and in provincial centres.'[12] The use of the word 'mainly' is significant. Despite references in his diary to the drudgery and the less pleasant aspects of his scientific work, it is evident from his notebooks and from letters he sent from Central Asia[13] that he took it seriously and prepared himself for it with considerably more enthusiasm than military duty alone demanded. Such a reaction was characteristic. Although he was no intellectual, he enjoyed reading for a practical purpose, and his interests, which were perhaps wider in scope than the usual cultural and artistic tastes of the cosmopolitan aristocracy to which he belonged, far exceeded those of the average officer.

He assimilated basic facts about the area from books by Przheval'skiy, Hedin and Stein; Kozlov, perhaps sensing a rival, was unwilling to share his knowledge. He approached Senator Otto Donner, the prominent Finnish scholar and initiator of several expeditions to Asia, to see what scientific information he could collect during his journey. Donner put him in touch with the Finno-Ugrian Society, which he joined, and with the Trustees of the Antell Collections in Helsinki. Thanks to these contacts in Finland he received a substantial brief to collect archaeological and ethnographic materials and manuscripts or fragments of them for the National Museum in Helsinki, to record inscriptions, and to study little-known tribes and peoples in northern China. This extended considerably the scope of his original plans. Afterwards he acknowledged modestly that if he had been able to contribute anything of value to science he owed it principally to two English text-books, *Hints to Travellers*, and *Notes and Queries on Anthropology*, 'which in a concentrated and lucid form provided the practical knowledge necessary for an explorer'.[14] He mastered them thoroughly, and his use of methods outlined in the latter is apparent in an article he published in 1911.[15] In addition, he learned how to take, develop and print photographs, and perfected his knowledge of the instruments needed for the mapping work that constituted one of his military tasks. He financed the expedition out of a grant from the General Staff and his pay, and borrowed money from

Sophie and Johan in anticipation of grants promised by the Antell Trustees, the Finno-Ugrian Society and the Secretariat of State for Finland.

After a frustrating fortnight calling on ministries and government offices in St. Petersburg, Mannerheim was given his papers on 6 July, 1906, and left the capital that evening on the night train to Moscow. The timing of his departure was in accordance with Pelliot's cabled instructions. As the two men discussed detailed arrangements in Tashkent, it quickly became clear to Mannerheim that the association with Pelliot was going to be unfortunate and would not afford the expected advantages of a secure background for his secret work and the benefit of sharing the knowledge of a traveller with experience of the area. Pelliot was put out because Mannerheim had not brought with him a grant of 10,000 francs Pelliot said he had been promised, or at least half promised. He was very annoyed to learn that the five Cossacks allocated for service with the expedition were to come under his authority through Mannerheim, who was, moreover, authorised to select two of them for his personal service. These two things combined to make Mannerheim's position in the expedition very different from what he had expected from the original discussions. After little more than two weeks' acquaintance with Pelliot he wrote to his father describing him as 'pettily stingy and grasping, jealous to the extreme of his dignity as head of the mission, a poseur, meddling in everything, an egoist to the highest degree'.[16] Mannerheim had already received an indication of Pelliot's meanness when the un-reasonable financial conditions he imposed prevented the implementation of Mannerheim's plan to take along his brother-in-law, Count Louis Sparre, Eva's husband, as artist to the expedition. Now Pelliot wanted him to pay a quarter of all expenses. A good many discussions had been necessary to establish his complete independence in all respects, and he intended to separate from Pelliot for most of the first year of the expedition since he was not interested in accompanying him to Lob Nor.

The discussions with Pelliot during the first stage of the journey were not concluded without concessions by Mannerheim. He noted in his report that he had felt obliged to ask Pelliot to make clear his position in the expedition because he was worried by the somewhat strange, and even hostile, attitude the Frenchman showed towards him and his work, which would obviously hamper him in carrying out his mission. Pelliot replied that the French Ministry of Foreign Affairs, having refused to grant Mannerheim a passport, asked him indirectly through the Russian ambassador to give his agreement to Mannerheim's participation in the expedition, thus underlining its unwillingness to accept responsibility for any difficulties that might ensue. He had agreed that Mannerheim should travel in company with him, but not as a member of the expedition, since the presence in it of a Russian officer, who would be working on his own and not subject to his control, might easily compromise the expedition in the eyes of the Chinese authorities. He would try not to betray Mannerheim to these authorities, but if they asked him a direct question he would have to give a straight reply. 'This answer, in the context of his patently unfriendly attitude towards me, made me realise that I could count on no help or support from him. This and a series of minor details of his character, on which I will not dwell, made my position in the expedition extremely awkward.'[17] Pelliot went so far as to say that he would probably not allow Mannerheim to reconnoitre the route through the Muzart Pass and carry out similar work near the Russian frontier.

It is not difficult to understand Pelliot's fear of losing the good-will of the Chinese on which his future work depended, but the fear took a practical form which constituted for Mannerheim a gross breach of faith. Nevertheless, to try to improve relations and to attain conditions under which he would be able to do his official work, Mannerheim undertook that he would embark on no excursion without previously consulting Pelliot, and that he would inform him of all the results of his work. He also in effect placed the Cossacks under Pelliot's orders and handed over to him all the money for their upkeep. In addition he included most of his supplies and equipment with Pelliot's. Even so, his hope of improving relations was unfortunately disappointed. To his annoyance, Pelliot spoke indiscreetly about his identity or work to the expedition's doctor, Major Louis Vaillant, and possibly the photographer, Charles Nouette, also got to know about it. The description of Mannerheim's nationality on the pass issued in Kashgar may have stemmed from a chance remark by one of the Frenchmen being overheard by their Chinese interpreter.[18] He travelled with Pelliot from Osh to Kashgar but separated from him there, no doubt thankfully. Travelling alone accorded better with his temperament and with the nature of his mission. However, he kept his word to remain in touch, and the two men exchanged many letters concerned with their results and plans. Attempts to meet again failed because Pelliot subsequently altered by as much as two months the dates he gave for a rendezvous with Mannerheim.

All reference to Pelliot was omitted from the version of Mannerheim's report published by the General Staff in its Collection of Geographical, Topographical and Statistical Materials Concerning Asia.[19] Although the report was intended for official use only, the series had a fairly wide circulation[20] and the omission was justifiable on security grounds – the Russians might want to attach an officer to another archaeological expedition at some future date. Moreover, there was nothing to be gained by revealing Pelliot in an unfavourable light and in risking prejudicing his relations with the Chinese. Kai Donner, in his biography of Mannerheim published in 1934, mentioned Mannerheim's association with Pelliot's expedition, and their separation after travelling together from Osh to Kashgar, though he gave no reason for it.[21] However Mannerheim chose not to mention Pelliot either in the published version of the diary of his expedition or in his memoirs.[22] These works, therefore, give a distorted picture of the preparations for the expedition, and also convey the false impression that Mannerheim made the journey from Osh to Kashgar alone. That Pelliot, who died in 1945, was still alive when the diary was published may perhaps have had some connection with the omission. Mannerheim, who was always careful to behave correctly, may have felt himself still bound by the considerations of security and prudence that had prevailed immediately after the expedition. It is possible, though not really likely, that he may have sought to emphasise his own achievement by ignoring Pelliot,[23] and it is possible, too, that he may have decided in this way to repay Pelliot for his lack of co-operation; Mannerheim had a long memory for grievances and the wrongs he had suffered.

On leaving St. Petersburg he made the first entry in the diary in which he was to record the progress of his expedition during the next two years. It was not written with any intention of publication in its original form, but the Finno-Ugrian Society learned that if the diary were to be published he would like it to be done by them. In the autumn of 1936 the Society secured his consent to its publication in connection with his forthcoming seventieth birthday celebrations. The work was to appear in English, necessitating the translation of the diary from its original Swedish. Kaarlo Hildén, Professor of Economic Geography at the Helsinki School of Economics, was appointed editorial secretary, and Mannerheim took great personal interest in the task, going carefully through the whole manuscript although official duties were making heavy demands on his time. He wanted to delete certain parts of the text, and was reluctant to let any references to his frequent ailments be published, on the grounds that they could be of no interest and that their inclusion might lead people to think that by stressing the difficulties of the journey he was emphasising his own physical endurance.[24] Mannerheim disliked intrusion into his private life, and this unwillingness to expose his own suffering was typical of the man, who destroyed much biographical material and long thought it reprehensible to write his memoirs. He looked over the English translation and even made various changes after composition had begun, 'to make the account more lively'.[25] As Commander-in-Chief during the Winter War it was difficult for him to find time to write a foreword, but at last the preface was signed and dated 'General Headquarters of the Finnish Army, February 1940', and the diary was published a few weeks later. A second volume, in which aspects of his work in Central Asia were examined by a group of scholars, appeared in the same year.

The manuscript material from Mannerheim's Asian expedition, preserved by the Finno-Ugrian Society,[26] comprises his diary in seven cloth-bound notebooks, a notebook listing routes, which also contains various continuations from the diary, and another notebook containing meteorological observations. Hildén commented that the diary was written clearly and beautifully throughout, and gave an impression of a fresh and polished style.[27] Mannerheim had attached great importance to good handwriting ever since he was a young boy, and his diary, written for the most part in black ink and with double spacing, is invariably clear, though the entries appear more hurriedly written towards the end. The presence of numerous emendations and insertions made at the time of writing detracts, however, from the over-all appearance, but the diary nevertheless remains an exceptionally fine manuscript. This is more remarkable when one considers the circumstances in which it was kept. The diary was compiled in smoky hovels, stifling rooms, freezing tents, sometimes with the hairs from the travelling rugs choking his nostrils and his pen. On 28 February, 1908, he noted that 'it grows irksome in the course of time to write up your diary daily and in the end you begin to look for pretexts for avoiding it now and then',[28] but he rarely failed to record events day by day, no matter how tired he was after perhaps a twelve-hour ride, and no matter how bad the conditions for writing were. The diary, as a source of his report, is a chronicle of the route, of dates, distances and places, and also includes much military and statistical material. There is a strong emphasis on factors affecting the

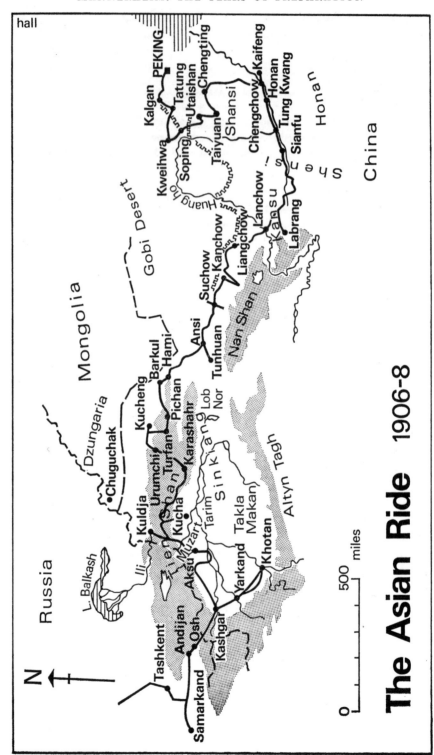

hall

The Asian Ride 1906-8

military capacity of the route, such as the availability of water, fodder and fuel, the condition of bridges, ferries and fords, the suitability of roads for wheeled traffic, particulars of the 'going' – marshy, stony, soft or hard – and of restrictions imposed by weather conditions. Slips of paper, still in the manuscript, listing the points he wished to cover in a particular entry, show the care with which he worked. But what gives the diary literary interest is the appearance, from time to time, among the facts, of a descriptive passage which reveals the author as a gifted writer as well as an extremely perceptive observer. The diary, written in the same warm, elegant and informative style as his letters to his family, is a far more human document than the deliberately impersonal memoirs, and from it emerges an indication of his personality.

Mannerheim travelled by train to Nizhniy Novgorod and by steamer down the Volga to Astrakhan. He crossed the Caspian Sea to Krasnavodsk and then continued by train to Tashkent, where he received a detailed briefing on routes and local conditions from the military staff. At Samarkand he collected the Ural Cossacks put at his disposal by order of the Emperor. He reached Andijan, the railhead, on 29 July, 1906, continuing by stage coach to Osh. After buying saddle- and pack-horses, engaging men and sorting their equipment, the expedition started out on 11 August, making for Kashgar in Sinkiang, an important trading centre 190 miles beyond the mountains. He crossed into China on 24 August and reached Kashgar six days later after hard marches that reduced the horses to a pitiful state. The secret reports shown to him by the Russian consul in Kashgar contained frequent references to the appearance of Japanese in Sinkiang, and to find out whether there were Japanese in southern Kashgaria he started south-east for Yarkand and Khotan on 6 October, travelling along the western edge of the Takla Makan desert. At Yarkand he suffered an attack of rheumatism which made him doubt seriously whether he would ever reach Khotan, but he did; his spirits revived and his head was full of plans. There was no trace of any Japanese.

He returned to Kashgar, which felt like returning to civilisation since it was the only place in the area where some European amenities were to be found and where there was lively social activity. On 27 January, 1907, he set out for Aksu, the most important military centre in western Sinkiang, 250 miles to the north-east, travelling first along the caravan route and later across roadless and waterless terrain, arriving on 2 March. The next stage took the expedition over the icy and perilous Muzart

Pass in the Tien Shan to Kuldja, where he spent a month putting his surveys and other work in order and obtaining supplies, personnel and permits. Leaving there on 4 May, he moved south-east across the Tien Shan to Karashahr, where he arrived on 5 July and wrote: 'It is only after two months' travel in the mountains in the cold, wind and rain, with no other food than rusks and mutton, that I have learned to rate the blessings of civilisation at their true value. . . . It was a pleasure to ride through tilled fields and populated districts.'[29] He continued back over the Tien Shan to Urumchi, the capital of the province of Sinkiang and an important military and commercial centre, which he reached on 24 July, badly needing to replenish his depleted purse. The presence of a Russian consul there, as at Kashgar and Kuldja, greatly simplified his administrative arrangements and helped him gain access to local officials, but Krotkov, the consul at Urumchi, though hospitable, was far less co-operative than Kolokolov at Kashgar or Fyodorov at Kuldja, and Mannerheim commented in a letter to his father on his 'jalousie de métier'.[30] He spent a month at Urumchi, occupied part of the time with formal calls on local dignitaries. The first year of the expedition had passed.

At the end of August he left Urumchi and reached Kucheng, the most northerly point of his ride, on 5 September. He recrossed the Tien Shan to Turfan, continuing over the northern slope of the mountains to Barkul, where he arrived on 12 October. Then he moved southwards across the Tien Shan for the sixth and last time to Hami, and crossed the Gobi desert to Ansi, a miserable town which he reached on 9 November. There was a good, if monotonous, road from Ansi to Suchow, which rose impressively from the almost bare bank of the river in front of the town. He spent some days there, half way between Kuldja and Peking, before moving on to Kanchow just before Christmas. After visiting two practically unknown Yögur tribes in the nearby mountains, he continued his march to Lanchow on 7 January, 1908, following the caravan road close to the Great Wall, with the Nan Shan to his right and the Gobi desert on his left. On the way he passed ruins dating from the suppression of the Dungan revolt. He arrived in Lanchow on the upper Hwang ho, the capital of Kansu province and a town of great strategic importance, on 29 January. From there he went to Hochow, the centre of an area inhabited by Dungans, going on to visit the Tibetan monastery at Labrang, where he was given a hostile reception, being hissed and stoned. He was stoned again by some lamas from a nearby monastery at Kadia and had to fire his shot-gun to disperse the crowd. He did not, however, encounter the bandits for which the desolate country was noted.

He resumed his main route from Lanchow to Sianfu, the capital of Shensi, where he arrived on 28 April after a journey of 450 miles. He reached Kaifeng, capital of Honan, 300 miles to the east, on 30 May, having travelled the last miles from Chenchow by train. He had now reached the civilised zone of China and continued northwards by rail to Taiyuan. From there he despatched most of his baggage to Peking, but went on himself to Utaishan monastery, where he was given an audience by the exiled Dalai Lama on 26 June. Members of the Dalai Lama's suite forcibly prevented a Chinese official, who was keeping Mannerheim under surveillance during his stay in Utaishan, from entering the audience chamber. It seemed the Dalai Lama, who appeared young and vigorous, full of interest in political events and with a lively mind, was waiting his chance to break free from the restraints the Chinese imposed on him in their attempt to make his reinstatement conditional on his recognition of the supremacy of their Emperor. He displayed great interest in Russia, wanting to know whether Mannerheim had come with a special message, and presented him with a beautiful piece of white silk for the Emperor. However, it was disappointing that he refused to be photographed. From Utaishan Mannerheim went north to Soping and reached Kweihwa on the borders of Mongolia on 4 July, the object of this movement being to check the intensity of Chinese colonisation in that area. He turned east to Tatung and north-east to Kalgan, where the diary ended on 20 July, 1908. The last part of the journey to Peking was by train; he arrived on 25 July.

As planned by the General Staff, the expedition had taken two years. During that time Mannerheim had passed from the oases of Chinese Turkestan, with their Turkic-speaking population then known as Sarts, into the desert and mountain zones inhabited by the nomadic Kirghiz and Kalmuk peoples, and then into China proper, crossing part of the loess highlands and entering the alluvial plains. It was a remarkable feat of endurance, both physical and mental. He had been ill several times – at Kashgar with sunstroke, with bouts of rheumatism, at Lanchow with a lung pain succeeded by neuralgia an official dinner in a draughty room. But he had recovered and pressed on. His Cossacks, who had been selected for their toughness, failed to come up to expectations. One was sent back from Kashgar for improper behaviour. The other, who had been seriously ill coming over the Muzart pass, was replaced at Kuldja on account of his unsatisfactory conduct by a third Cossack, Lukanin, who proved an excellent helper. However, his health had become badly weakened towards the end of the journey and he was sent direct to Peking from Taiyuan in charge of the baggage.

Capable men, who could free Mannerheim from trivial jobs and thus allow him to carry out his work, were hard to find. He set out with four Sarts, a Chinese interpreter and a servant, in addition to his two Cossacks, but the size of the caravan fluctuated somewhat as the journey went on. He acquired a good cook, 'a master of his art', but could not keep him the whole time and sometimes had to endure indifferent food. Bad interpreters were a constant handicap and irritation, and it was as well he learned some Chinese. 'You seldom get an answer to your questions and are forced to stand and listen to a great deal of unnecessary chatter, from which you have to draw your own conclusions.'[31] He stressed in his report that it was impossible to secure any kind of satisfactory interpreters, either in Russian or in Chinese Turkestan. Occasionally the drivers did not turn up, adding to his problems and disrupting his timetable. Near Suchow he thrashed the wrong man for being late, an injustice he attempted to put right with a good tip.

The monotonous uniform greyness and the filth of Central Asia made a deep impression on him, and the discomfort and hardship of the journey were considerable. There were dangers, too. Without knowing it, he once slept on the edge of a precipice, and spent another night on a leper's bed. He was nearly swept away when fording a swollen river and had to fight for his life on the slippery boulders of the river bed. His horse grew accustomed to the sight of the skeletons and corpses of men and beasts that had perished from cold or hunger or had fallen in the treacherous country. The local people, apart from the nomads, were sometimes unwelcoming, though hostility such as he encountered at Labrang was exceptional. The attitude of the Chinese varied. At Aksu the authorities had helped by arranging, in return for payment, fuel and fodder along his route. The mandarins at Kuldja were obliging and paid great attention to the wishes of the Russians, who had a consulate there and troops to guard it, but the local Chinese population was distinctly antagonistic towards Russians. Chinese in regular contact with Europeans were keen to provoke them, and he heard many accounts from Europeans of atrocities committed during the Boxer rebellion.

He accepted the unpleasant side of the expedition with an ironical sense of humour. In Fencheng-ting on 12 July, 1908, he wrote: 'A traveller coming from the east, from China's more beautiful towns, might, perhaps, be struck by the stench and filth of the streets, which are often low-lying, but a nose such as mine, hardened in Central Asia and Western China, is not worried by such a bagatelle.'[32] On arriving in Kuldja, 'I was preparing to make my room in the sarai look cosy and home-like, with my shabby felt boots, filthy clothes, a broken compass, a cracked glass, a creaking bed, etc., when an aksakal [a local agent] from the Russian consul arrived with the suggestion that I should put up in the house of a rich Sart horsedealer opposite the Cossack guard of the consulate. Naturally, I was delighted to accept this offer.'[33] The occasional good bed was not the only pleasure. The magnificence of the scenery, a patch of green in the grey wilderness, the delight of returning to a busy town after weeks in mountains or deserts, all gave pleasure to the traveller. It was an especial joy to see two small rosy-cheeked Nordic girls who spoke Swedish. He was naturally pleased to encounter other Europeans, but most of them were missionaries, many Swedish or Swedish-American protestants, who were generally too uneducated and uninteresting for his taste. He was more impressed by the spartan simplicity and devoted work of the incomparably better-educated Roman Catholic missionaries. Letters from home reached him from time to time at the main centres and in some places he received a bundle of newspapers as well as welcome post. However, he naturally felt very isolated and only on arriving at the Russian legation in Peking did he find 'what I had been missing throughout my long travels, pleasant people to talk with'.[34]

He spent some days in a district which 'may well be called a paradise, not only for sportsmen, but for all who love beautiful and grand scenery and enjoy the exertion entailed by an outdoor life'.[35] Mannerheim was such a man. He went shooting when he could, but his mapping work, to his chagrin, forced him to overcome the constant temptation the sight of game represented. Steep climbing in the mountains was trying to his legs, broken three times, but it was worth the pain to shoot his first ibex. His enthusiasm is very obvious. 'The neighbourhood is simply alive with pheasants. During the day I shot seven fine cocks, one of them brought down with my Browning while mounted, and a bird of prey streaked with white.'[36] Shooting successes meant, too, a welcome change in the monotonous diet. The condition of the horses was of vital importance to the success of the expedition and horses were, as always, one of his major interests. 'It was a real pleasure to see such plentiful and harmonious material' in a stud owned by a Kalmuk. He joined eagerly in the Kirghiz sport of wrestling on horseback for the carcass of a goat and once succeeded in getting it on his saddle. Forty years old, he was at the peak of his powers. A Finnish writer has remarked that the achievements of his expedition revealed with what inward richness he lived during these two years in Asia, so far from the honour and responsibility of his later life.[37]

Arrived in Peking, Mannerheim settled down to write a draft of his report, an essential but formidable task he regarded as tedious in the extreme. The Russian legation put at his disposal a pavilion in its gardens, but work was difficult in the debilitating heat, and he was further distracted by the need to pay calls on members of the numerous Russian colony in the city. He aimed to complete a short account in about two weeks, but the fortnight stretched to about six weeks, and the short account became a substantial document of some 130–150 typewritten sheets. Despite the vastness of the region he had crossed, the problems posed by inefficient interpreters and the secrecy with which the Chinese surrounded all statistics, his report, with its appendices, reveals how much political, military, and economic information he had been able to collect through careful enquiries backed by meticulous observation. His thoroughness in this respect is perhaps most clearly evident from the tables in his diary showing the administrative subdivisions of the districts through which he had passed, the names of the villages with their area and tax assessment, the approximate size of the population, the numbers of domestic animals and the yield of the crops. After sifting and assessing the detail he had amassed, he was able to draw a broad picture of the region which, though inevitably imperfect, supplemented the reports from the legation and the consulates and provided in addition a more detailed and specialist analysis of areas where there was no Russian representation.

Members of the Russian legation in Peking found the draft of the report interesting; he considered it dry and boring. His judgment was certainly too harsh. Its vocabulary is considerably richer than that usually employed in military writings, and the style has individuality. Although naturally more restrained than the diary or his private letters, descriptions of terrain, people and places are often completed by an agreeable phrase, and he permitted himself a few expressions of personal feeling, such as his reaction to listening to the sound of the distant whistle of a locomotive at Chenchow, 'with more enthusiasm than I had ever listened in the past to the delicate sounds of an opera'. As completed in St. Petersburg, the report amounted to 192 typewritten foolscap pages.[38] The first part consisted of a summary of the journey and an outline of the development of reforms in China. The second part dealt with specific topics – railway construction, military forces, schools, industry and mining, the influence of the Japanese, and colonisation, ending with an assessment of the prospects for further reform. The appended maps, reconnaissance and statistical material completed the report and constituted 'the main result of my journey'.[39]

Mannerheim recognised the conflict going on within the court at Peking between the conservatives and the progressives, the influence of the former gradually fading away before the demands of the masses and the rapidly growing forces of public opinion in southern China. The central government, though stopping short of reforms threatening the traditional structure of the state, had given viceroys and governors a series of apparently similar directives, the more important of which related to railway construction in the provinces, the reorganisation of the army, the exploitation, at the expense of the treasury, of local mineral resources, and the development of industry, the opening of schools, the suppression of opium smoking, and the improvement of order in the towns. These directives were being carried out everywhere but without equal consistency and precision. The broad independence enjoyed by the provincial authorities meant that in one province the reorganisation of the army might be started and in another the provision of schools, while other reforms were neglected completely. Such independence would become an advantage, he believed, when the progressives were generally in control, since it provided the administrator 'with the possibility of developing his own initiative widely and fearlessly in conformance with the local conditions and as guided by his own personal ideas'.[40]

After meeting senior and junior officials in the towns along his route, Mannerheim could mention the names and discuss the character and aspirations of the important initiators of reform in the northern provinces, and also explain their difficulties in dealing with the vast majority of the mandarins whose financial interest in the old system made them strong opponents of change. But he had also made himself familiar with the views of people of various social circles and with their attitude towards the reforms. The population of northern China, unlike that of the south, was not imbued with the reformist spirit and was not inwardly in sympathy with innovations. But they were also apathetic and lacking in solidarity: there was no basis for a clash between the people and the authorities there. The north Chinese would follow the path of reform, along which the authorities had somewhat hesitantly set out, without loud discontent or enthusiasm. The mass of the Sart population in Sinkiang hated their Chinese rulers, but was too passive and apathetic to rise against them: in the event of a war there they would remain spectators. The Dungans of Kansu on the other hand, still constituted a restless element who might be roused to revolt, especially on the issue of religion.

The events of the Russo-Japanese War, together with the disturbances in Russia and the commencement of military reform in China, had shaken belief in Central Asia in Russia's invincible might. The mandarins in the frontier regions, who were very interested in developments in Russia, felt calmer in consequence, but still showed themselves suspicious and out of sympathy with Russia. Ill-will and discontent were particularly strong in the Ili region, exacerbated by the commercial privileges enjoyed by Russian Sart merchants and by the way the Russians had cut strips off the district for their own advantage – a process on which Mannerheim declined to comment, but which he criticised by implication. He even observed unmistakeable signs of dissatisfaction and anger among the population of Russian Turkestan, where the rapid rise in economic prosperity, which contrasted so powerfully with the misery of Chinese Turkestan, had not made the people well disposed towards the Russians. 'In the enthusiasm of his national awakening the Russian Sart sees those who have subjugated his country as his oppressors, and it does not even occur to him that he owes the progress which he has achieved mainly to the many millions which we have contributed each year to the budget of his country. There is still less indication of any attraction towards us on the part of the population of Chinese Turkestan.'[41] However, except among a few patent Japanophiles, there was no evidence of sympathy for Japan, and although Japanese activity in northern China, primarily as teachers, had increased noticeably during the previous two or three years, they inspired apprehension and distrust. The mandarins in particular hated them, and the Chinese undoubtedly preferred the Russians to the Japanese.

The implementation of reform had made considerably more progress in the provinces to the east than in Sinkiang, where little had been accomplished. Reform was, however, everywhere handicapped by two major obstacles – lack of people and lack of means. Difficulties in the execution of the railway construction plan and in the proposed development of industry and mining exemplified these obstacles. The central government was determined to prevent the establishment of foreign influence in the economy and therefore refused to grant any more concessions to foreign firms. Finding capital internally was difficult. Each province was supposed to finance the railways passing through it, but because the projects were in the hands of the mandarins, merchants and capitalists were suspicious of them and unwilling to subscribe to railway shares. An additional land tax levied in Shensi to cover the cost of railway construction was cancelled by the central government after local complaints against a non-traditional impost. Having failed to accumulate the necessary capital, the provincial administrations generally failed to study how to carry out the railway projects; little surveying was done, and costings were far too low to allow for construction in difficult terrain. Lack of capital also hampered the development of industry and mining, but in any case the mineral resources could not be fully exploited until the transportation problem was solved by the construction of railways. The rate of railway building would depend on the willingness of the government to contract foreign loans, the only remaining means of raising the large sums required. All enterprise was restricted by the acute shortage of technicians, and some provincial authorities were reluctant to call in foreign experts, though they were employed with success in Kansu and Shensi.

The lack of people trained in the western manner that was holding up the development of the country was being gradually remedied by the accomplishment of the programme of educational reform. This programme, which had been thought out intelligently and on a broad scale and was closely linked to the practicalities of life, was making progress in the northern provinces in proportion to their distance from Peking, a pattern that was repeated in all other fields of reform. In two years or so 30,000–40,000 schools had been opened throughout the Empire, a remarkable achievement and a reflection of the government's heavy expenditure on education. The quality of the teaching was often poor, but the return of the many Chinese studying abroad, particularly in Japan, would improve the general level of knowledge and ability. It was to be hoped, too, that those Chinese who qualified abroad would bring back the virtues of incorruptibility and impartiality so wanting in the administration of the country. Specialist schools concerned, for example, with agriculture, mining, commerce and railways, were as yet mostly specialising only on paper. However, cadet corps had been established to produce much-needed officers, and the curriculum of all upper schools included some military training. School reform, though far from complete, had struck roots which could not be pulled up. Indeed, the same could be said of the reform movement as a whole, and an awakened and revived China was no longer just a possibility but a fact.

The future of China nevertheless remained uncertain. Unless financial reform was given first priority, the country would not be restored as a great power in spite of the increasing strength of the progressive element, the growth of national consciousness in the masses and the commencement of reforms. Fundamental change in the field of finance at the centre was held up by the government's uncertainty of how to smash the traditions of the past without stirring up the whole of the administrative service against it. Mannerheim concluded his report with a question. 'Will the Chinese reformers succeed, inspired, as they are, with genuine patriotism and supported by the sympathy of the popular masses, in now smashing the resistance of the crowd of cunning mandarins, hanging on for dear life to the old system of financial administration which made them rich in the past, and which has already brought China to the brink of disaster, or will the adherents of the old regime be triumphant?'[42]

The military results of the expedition were considerable and significant. Mannerheim compiled extensive and detailed military statistical material about the whole of his route, and in particular the Aksu oasis, and combined reports of the strength and distribution of Chinese army units with a careful assessment of their fighting potential. In general, the efficiency of the army increased as he went east. 'The picture which I saw during my travels round Chinese Turkestan was, for a soldier, an extremely sad one. In 1906–7 the military reforms had barely touched the Sinkiang province. It was in Urumchi only that there were organised units in which they had started to introduce the new service requirements.'[43] In Kashgaria, and in the detachments stationed on the roads along the Tien Shan, the old military system prevailed unaffected by the new regulations and instructions sent to the officers there. Units were well below strength and up to a third of their personnel were physically incapable of bearing arms. The garrison of Yarkand appeared to be 'a regular gang of criminals, opium smokers, professional gamblers, usurers, owners of disreputable houses, etc.'[44] The old training system, which included fencing with an imaginary opponent, was often carried out badly or not at all. More attention was paid to shooting, but the results varied. The worst troops of all, those at Barkul, did not even do any shooting: they were engaged principally in farming. No manoeuvres or tactical training were carried out anywhere, and there were no sappers or medical personnel. The armament of the troops was varied and frequently unserviceable. Reserves of ammunition were small, but equipment was on order to expand the cartridge manufacturing capacity of the arsenal at Urumchi. The new field units (*lutszyun*) formed in 1906 at Urumchi were nearly up to strength but the principal result of two years' training was proficiency in marching and gymnastics.

In Kansu and Shensi the position was better then in Sinkiang, though not so good as in Honan and Shansi, from which the provincial militia (*chipin*) had practically disappeared. The militia in Kansu and Shensi, armed with match-locks, was of no military value. The 'field troops for dealing with internal enemies' (*syubey fantszyun*) were improving, particularly near the provincial capitals and in Shensi. Trained on the same lines as the new field troops, though not comparable with them in efficiency because of their distribution on patrol work, they were of a higher standard in Honan and Shansi. The new field troops themselves in Kansu and Shensi did not yet include cavalry. They did little shooting and no tactical training, but a great deal of close order drill and gymnastics. The new troops everywhere showed great virtuosity in marching and drill and the standard of their gymnastics was superb. There was a brigade of these troops, one of which included sappers, in each of the provincial capitals of Honan and Shansi. Duties were strictly observed and the Honan brigade even carried out manoeuvres in the autumn. Nevertheless, the striking feature of the new field troops was the absence of the most important aspects of military training. They were indifferent towards range work and the artillery did no firing. The cavalry did hardly any drill mounted. Tactical training, including movement in open order and the use of ground, was completely neglected.

The Chinese had at their disposal a number of additional military and para-military forces and tribal levies. Foremost of these were the garrisons of Manchu troops. Although generally unsympathetic to the reforms, which upset their traditional privileges, the Manchu garrisons in Kaifeng and Taiyuan were up to the standard of the new field troops, and the reorganisation of other garrisons was in progress or planned. The mobility of the field units would be facilitated considerably by the existence, especially in the more easterly towns, of numerous police detachments, organised on military lines. The nomad tribes were a source of irregular troops and Mannerheim often witnessed the conscription of their members for military service. The Kirghiz, who paid a small property tax, did not consider themselves liable for military service but did some frontier patrolling. The Kalmuks and Tanguts accepted that the Chinese could call up a definite number of men, with their own arms and horses, in the event of war. Military service for the Mongol tribes was, however, 'of a purely platonic character',[45] and though supposed to be able to find tens of thousands of armed horsemen, they were unable to turn out any trained cavalry. The Chinese could, nevertheless, create a considerable force of real cavalry from the Mongols if they paid them. Such a force would be particularly valuable in the vast semi-desert areas and would be able to dispute matters successfully with the Russian Cossacks.

The immediate objectives of the army reorganisation had been declared to be: to secure the most threatened border regions against the external enemy, to ensure order within the country, and to develop the armed forces sufficiently for the recovery of border districts which had at some time been lost. Sinkiang, China's western front, was admitted to be one of the most threatened border districts, and it had been decided to form one division there by 1907, and two divisions in Kansu by 1913. Later, the formation of the second division in Kansu was cancelled in favour of a special division for the Ili region. It was unlikely that these two divisions in Sinkiang would be formed by the appointed time and the units already on the spot, the cadres for further formations, were not yet properly trained. Although the men were excellent material, quick to grasp their jobs, and with great energy and immense powers of endurance that one would not suspect from their puny appearance, the officers and staff of the high command were unsatisfactory. There was an acute shortage of officers which the recently founded lower-grade cadet corps would not properly remedy, and in spite of good personal qualities in many cases, the officers lacked the knowledge to bring their troops up to modern standards.

Other factors contributed to the extremely weak defensive capacity of Sinkiang and precluded the possibility of offensive moves against Russian territory. Communications with the rest of China were poor and the delivery of munitions and other supplies from the interior could not be guaranteed. This was particularly serious because of the varied and defective armament of the troops in Sinkiang, the insufficiency of reserves of ammunition there, and the inability of the province to produce a surplus of foodstuffs large enough to support additional troops. The unreliability of the native population forced the government to rely for recruits almost exclusively on the Chinese minority, which was growing only slowly through colonisation. Trained reserves were non-existent and could be created only with difficulty. In four or five years, however, the situation might become very different, with a well-trained and well-equipped army of two to three divisions in Sinkiang, while in thirteen to fifteen years, or even sooner, the western front might be linked by railway to the rest of the Empire. Mannerheim appreciated the implications of this. 'Such a prospect, in its turn, makes us wonder to what extent the condition of our armed forces and of the railway system in the belt adjacent to western China will then correspond to the tasks which will be incumbent upon it in the event of a clash with China.'[46]

Mannerheim devoted several pages of his report to an interesting assessment of the importance of Sinkiang in the context of a war between Russia and China. He saw the province as a secondary theatre of operations which it would be rash of the Russians to ignore since the Chinese troops there, without a rail link with the rest of China, were in a hopeless position.

'The success of our action in this province could not, of course, have any decisive effect on the course of the war, but it would draw off 3-4 divisions (those of Sinkiang, Kansu, Ili and perhaps Shensi). The annexation to our Asiatic possessions of this very extensive territory, with a sparse population and vast deserts, would hardly interest us, except as regards the Ili district and perhaps a few more small parts, but Sinkiang province in our hands at the time when peace was declared would surely be an inestimably weighty argument, regardless of the result of operations in the main, i.e. the Manchurian, theatre of war.'[47]

It was obvious that Mannerheim appreciated the political significance of military action. The plan of operations he suggested was designed to achieve the political aim of seizing Sinkiang, and he was not tempted to pursue further operations which would be militarily difficult and yield no political advantage.

He considered that Urumchi, the chief administrative and military centre of Sinkiang, should be the objective of a Russian invasion. If they advanced from Chuguchak, the Russians would cut the communications of the troops in Ili and weaken their defensive capacity. To ensure the success of operations near Urumchi, it would be desirable to cut communications between Sinkiang and the rest of China by seizing Hami and

Barkul. This task could be carried out by a strong force of cavalry, with horse artillery and machine guns, moving out through the Tekes and Yulduz valleys and the towns of Kashgar, Turfan and Pichan, but it was possible only between May and September when the passes were open. The only opposition on entering the Tekes valley would be from small frontier units of Kalmuks, and Chinese troops would not be encountered until the Russians entered the Kunges valley. Kashgar could be taken easily and its possession would isolate the Chinese garrisons in the southern part of Sinkiang so that no further account need be taken of them. A clash might occur with detachments from Urumchi around Toksun and Turfan, particularly if the Russian force did not advance along the northern slope of the Tien Shan with sufficient energy. In winter, an attack on Hami could only be carried out through the Urumchi region and then via Kucheng or Turfan. The capture of Urumchi would mark the end of a major operation on the western front. By occupying Hami and advancing a small detachment to Kucheng, the Russians would be able to hinder Chinese attempts to recover the province.

It is noteworthy that Mannerheim's plan to capture Urumchi and isolate Sinkiang from the rest of China involved a bold, deeply-penetrating cavalry movement, which nevertheless took careful account of the limitations imposed on offensive action by the terrain, climate, and the shortage of water and other supplies in the region. But having achieved his limited political objective, his boldness turned to caution: he saw no point, and no advantage, in advancing further. It was possible to advance on Suchow, but there, and around Kanchow and Lianchow, the Russians would encounter three detachments, each of several battalions and squadrons, protected by the massive walls of the towns. In Lanchow they would clash with the main force of the army of Kansu. Russian communications would be extended across a desert area through which supplies would have to be moved along poor roads. The advance from Urumchi would take infantry not less than 5–6 months. The result of this massive effort, the capture of Lanchow, would be a blow to China, but not a decisive one since Lanchow was strategically important only in relation to Kansu. Until the construction of the Sianfu–Lanchow–Urumchi railway, Lanchow could not be considered a base for Chinese troops in Sinkiang. Its possession by the Russians did not constitute a threat to Peking since an advance in that direction could be easily blocked. Further advance, towards Peking or towards Sianfu and the Peking–Hankow railway, would entail movement across enormous distances. 'The ultimate aim of our war with China could be achieved in a shorter time, and certainly with less effort, by the destruction of the Chinese army in the main theatre, i.e. in Manchuria.'[48] More serious difficulties could be created for the Chinese government with the expenditure of less effort. Although it would not succeed, it would be possible to raise a Dungan revolt, assisted by bodies of Russian volunteers and with Russian arms, provided the Russians established close relations with the most influential Dungans during peace-time. Similar relations should be cultivated with the Sarts and Mongols, with the object of inciting them to revolt and to form units under Russian officers. In these respects, too, Mannerheim showed a clear realisation of the significance of non-military factors in war plans. His outline of operations was realistic in its appreciation, vigorous in its execution, and prudent in its strategy.

He compiled valuable maps to supplement his description of the journey and his military appreciation. Parts of his route were familiar to Europeans, but several sections of his ride took him through country, either imperfectly known or totally unexplored, about which the Russian General Staff wanted detailed information. He therefore presented with his report a map, at a scale of 1 : 84,000, covering approximately 2,300 miles of his route. The compilation of this map, carried out in all weathers, had been a laborious task, which had involved noting the distance covered and making continual observations with compass and barometer. The surveys were made in notebooks, and at first he transcribed them on to plotting boards either at each halt or during stays in towns. This 'niggling task' took up so much time that eventually he left it to be done at the end of the journey.[49] The complete route mapping was revised and published at a scale of 1 : 200,000 in 1940 as part of the companion volume to his diary: its editor commented on 'the plastic beauty, with which it left his hands'.[50] In addition to the route map, he prepared several town plans at a scale of 1 : 42,000. These were provided with full descriptions and notes, paying particular attention to the state of the fortifications, covered lines of approach, and the location of important buildings. He also produced maps of communications in Kansu and Shansi, of railway projects, of the distribution of troops and of tribes, and a detailed survey of part of the river Taushkan-Darya. He had been constantly recording map corrections and pointed out that the maps of northern Shansi were particularly poor. The small scale (100 verst) map of China published by the General Staff was too incorrect for him to be able to sketch his route on it with absolute accuracy.

Mannerheim's military work revealed the capacity of his intellect; his scientific observations, for which he had not been trained, revealed also its versatility. He kept a daily meteorological record, conducted archaeological excavations, copied ancient inscriptions and collected objects illustrating the life and culture of Central Asian peoples, notably the Sarts. These activities were sometimes trying when there was so much else to be done. He complained that 'such unproductive labour' as repairing broken cases, packing and labelling the things he had bought, 'takes up a great deal of time and poisons the life of an unfortunate traveller'.[51] But he persisted and what mistakes and omissions he made can be attributed to inexperience. For example, he took no precise details of thermometer corrections and failed to have control measurements of the barometers made on his return.[52] But his work was of a remarkably high standard: second best was never good enough for him, whatever he was doing. Kai Donner, an authority on linguistics who was well qualified to judge, commented that the list of Yögur words appended to the article Mannerheim published on the Sarö and Shera Yögurs[53] was a proof of his ability to make accurate linguistic observations and notes which were, moreover, important to experts.[54] It was unfortunate that the täzkirs, sacred documents he bought in Southern Kashgaria, failed to confirm the local tradition of the origin of the Abdal beggar tribe, as had been hoped, but they proved of value in other respects. Among the manuscript fragments he acquired was one written in Mongolian quadratic script which provided scholars with new orthographical evidence.

His anthropological notes were not extensive and were unevenly distributed, but his material on the Abdals and the Sarö and Shera Yögurs was of great interest. Even by 1940 the anthropological particulars he had taken of the Sarö and Shera Yögurs appeared to be the only ones in existence. In all, he took anthropological measurements of 165 men from eight different peoples, a complicated procedure which took at least half an hour for each person and was anything but appetizing. 'The cleanliness of the Kirghiz leaves a good deal to be desired, but he seems almost aristocratic in comparison with the Kalmuk, whose filth exceeds the wildest dreams of the imagination.'[55] The ethnographic collections relating to the Sarts and Tibetans and various other peoples were valuable additions to the National Museum of Finland then being formed. The archaeological excavations were unimportant: he had little time to spare for such work and in any case lacked the necessary specialised knowledge. Mannerheim would have liked to have returned to Europe by sea, either around Asia or across America and England, but had neither time nor money to do so, and had to travel by rail across Siberia instead. He did, however, manage to fit in an eight days' visit to Japan before leaving the Far East. On 8 October, 1908, he was back in St. Petersburg and reported to the General Staff. He was then summoned to give an account of his expedition to the Emperor. Such an audience was a great honour and he faced it with a certain trepidation. He enquired how long his account should take, and the Emperor told him twenty minutes would be sufficient. The Emperor rarely received a first-hand report on conditions in Central Asia and his questions and comments indicated that he was listening attentively. He accepted the Dalai Lama's gift with outstretched hands, in the traditional manner. 'A glance at a clock showed me that what I had thought was a short account had taken an hour and twenty minutes, whereupon I humbly apologized for the length of my report. The Emperor smilingly thanked me for an interesting account, and said that he, also, had failed to notice how time went.' The Emperor asked him what his plans were. Now the journey was over Mannerheim had begun to fear the long absence would have an adverse effect on his military career, and he expressed his concern that he might have missed promotion, and his hope that he might soon command a regiment. The Emperor reassured him and pointed out that few men had been privileged to undertake such a task. 'I later realized how true this was.'[56]

Mannerheim's achievement certainly impressed the Emperor, who spoke about it with keen interest and admiration to Sven Hedin at an audience in January 1909, advising Hedin to get in touch with him as soon as possible.[57] It became clear to Mannerheim that his work was well received. After completing the report in St. Petersburg – it was dated 31 October – he was able to write with satisfaction that people felt particularly pleased with the result of his journey. The Chief of the General Staff was evidently satisfied and his rapid advancement was assured. He nevertheless took good care and considerable trouble to ensure that he recovered his place on the list of officers awaiting command of a regiment. He received a regimental command in the New Year and thoughts of a career as an explorer were abandoned. He had realised how much work had already been done in Central Asia, writing rather disconsolately to his father from Kuldja on 7 April, 1907, that the materials he had collected in Chinese Turkestan would be of undoubted value 'if the country had not been so traversed by explorers in all fields, even the military. It now seems to me I am only poking into long known facts, though they are indeed interesting and were unknown to me until now.'[58] Later on, his painful lumbago forced him to conclude that he was in any case getting too old for new expeditions.

The secret military character of the journey and Mannerheim's occupation with the command of a regiment so soon after his return precluded the publication of much material about it. In 1909 the Russian General Staff printed for official use his preliminary account of the expedition.[59] This work did not reproduce the mapping and other appendices and was, of course, never translated. In 1911 the Finno-Ugrian Society published in its journal a 72-page article by Mannerheim about the Sarö and Shera Yögurs.[60] Based on entries in his diary, it included some anthropological measurements and a list of Yögur words, and was illustrated with a few of the 1,500 photographs taken during the journey. He pointed out in the preface, dated Helsingfors, August 10, 1909, that 'as the principal aim of my expedition lay altogether outside the spheres of anthropology and ethnography, and as I have had no opportunity to revise my more or less casually made observations, it is without the least claim to authority that I present this very unpretentious material to the kind consideration of the reader'.[61] A brief, but prompt, note of his return appeared in the geographical monthly report in *Petermanns Mitteilungen* completed on 29 May, 1909: 'After an absence of two years a Finnish scholar, Baron G. v. Monnerheim [*sic*] has returned to Helsingfors from Central Asia and the northern provinces of China proper. From Kashgar he crossed the Tien Shan three times, passed along the edge of the Gobi, visited Lanchow, the capital of Kansu, touched the eastern part of Tibet and arrived at Kalgan and Peking along the Hwang-ho through Shansi. His cartographic work comprises about 1,000 km.'[62] That was the extent of contemporary knowledge of his expedition.

In the preface to his diary, published in 1940, Mannerheim claimed: 'For want of time I have had to postpone from year to year the fulfilment of my original intention of preparing the notes made on the journey for publication.'[63] It is difficult to believe he had no time between 1919 and 1931 when he held no office and took no active part in Finnish political life. Although an account of the expedition had appeared in Donner's biography in 1934, it was true, as Hildén wrote, that, 'pour le grand public, *l'explorateur* Mannerheim n'existait pas'.[64] 'Mannerheim as an explorer' was a theme that Hildén and others were to develop, and it became part of the public image of the Marshal.[65] Sven Hedin, reviewing the diary, commented that it assured for its author 'a place of honour in the exploration of a great continent, a place of honour which in reality belonged to him thirty years ago'.[66]

Mannerheim's achievement in overcoming the physical obstacles presented by the journey, his courage in penetrating into unknown and little-known regions, and his initiative in carrying out scientific work entitle him to be described as an explorer. Finnish writers emphasised these aspects of his expedition because of their appeal as a story of adventure, and they stressed his scientific work because it was carried out for the benefit of Finnish organisations. Attention was thus diverted from his controversial service in the imperial army which formed the context of the journey. To set his exploration in proper perspective it is necessary to recall the secret nature of his task and his own comments on his 'casually made observations' and his 'unpretentious material' collected 'mainly with the object of making my work look scientific to my fellow travellers and to the Chinese authorities'. His real achievement lay in producing for the Russian General Staff useful answers to the questions that had prompted his mission. His report constituted a skilful description and appreciation of the state of the Chinese provinces through which he had passed, revealing his ability to produce a clear analysis of complicated problems, and proving – if proof were needed – that he was more than a conscientious officer with a devotion to horses and sport. There can be no doubt that the information he collected would have been invaluable to the Russians in the event of a war with China during the years immediately following his journey. The decision to send him, and his decision to go, had been amply justified.

REFERENCES

1. C. G. E. Mannerheim, *Predvaritel'nyy otchet o poyezdke predprinyatoy po Vysochay-shemu poveleniyu cherez Kitayskiy Turkestan i severnyya provintsii Kitaya v g. Pekin v 1906–7 i 8 g.g.*
(Preliminary account of an expedition carried out on orders from the sovereign through Chinese Turkestan and the northern provinces of China to Peking in the years 1906–7 and 1908.) p. 1. Duplicated (typewritten) MS. Valtionarkisto. Langhoffin kokoelma, XIV, No. 111. This copy is of the text of the report only. Mannerheim, *Memoirs*, p. 25, shows his surprise at the suggestion.
2. Ignat'yev, *A Subaltern in Old Russia*, pp. 281–2.
3. Jägerskiöld, *Gustaf Mannerheim*, pp. 13–14.
4. Mannerheim, *Predvaritel'nyy otchet*, pp. 1–2.

5. Mannerheim, *Predvaritel'nyy otchet*, p. 1. *Bulletin du Comité de L'Asie française*, 5, Paris, 1905, p. 288. *Ibid.*, p. 370. *Geographical journal*, 27, London, 1906, p. 87. *Ibid.*, 35, 1910, p. 594-5.

6. C. G. Mannerheim, *Across Asia*, i, p. 113. The description of his nationality and name in the diary ends with the comment: 'Such precision . . . is not the work of any Chinese in Kashgar.' A few days earlier the official who issued the pass had not known what a 'Finn' meant. Mannerheim did not mention the description of his nationality in his report, only his Chinese name. He later stated that the document from Peking had been requested in the name of 'the Finnish subject Mannerheim, travelling under the protection of the Russian government', but that it had not arrived and the pass with the Chinese name was arranged instead on the advice of the Russian consul. Mannerheim, *Memoirs*, p. 33.

7. Mannerheim, *Memoirs*, p. 33. The Chinese name is also given as 'the horse that jumped over the stars'. Mannerheim, *Predvaritel'nyy otchet*, p. 23.

8. Ignat'yev, *A Subaltern in Old Russia*, p. 281.

9. Mannerheim, *Predvaritel'nyy otchet*, p. 14. He kept the diary in New Style dating.

10. India Office. *Political and Secret Letters from India*, 1906/194, no. 1833. Diary and abstract of news reports [from Kashgar], 10.ix.1906. *Ibid.*, 1907/199, no. 603. Abstract of news reports [from Kashgar], 20.i.1907.

11. For example, *Political and Secret Letters from India*, 1907/197, no. 293. Abstract of news reports [from Kashgar], 10.xii.1906.

12. Mannerheim, *Predvaritel'nyy otchet*, p. 26. Although some of his excursions may have been undertaken for scientific reasons, e.g. the visit to the Sarö and Shera Yögurs, the scope of his orders was so wide that it is impossible to be certain. The main lines of his route were, of course, laid down by the General Staff.

13. For example, letters to Senator Otto Donner quoted by Jägerskiöld, *Gustaf Mannerheim*, pp. 42-5, and by Donner, *Sotamarsalkka vapaaherra Mannerheim*, pp. 32-7.

14. Mannerheim, *Memoirs*, p. 28. Edward Ayearst Reeves, *ed.*, *Hints to Travellers*, 9th ed., London, 1906, 2 vols. John George Garson and Charles Hercules Read, *ed.*, *Notes and Queries on Anthropology*, 2nd ed., London, 1892.

15. C. G. E. Mannerheim, 'A visit to the Sarö and Shera Yögurs', *Suomalais-ugrilaisen seuran aikakauskirja*, 27, ii, Helsinki, 1911. See above p. 84.

16. To Carl Robert Mannerheim, 9.viii.1906, quoted by Jägerskiöld, *Gustaf Mannerheim*, p. 31.

17. Mannerheim, *Predvaritel'nyy otchet*, p. 5.

18. Jägerskiöld, *Gustaf Mannerheim*, p. 21.

19. C. G. E. Mannerheim, *Predvaritel'nyy otchet o poyezdke, predprinyatoy po Vysochayshemu poveleniyu cherez Kitayskiy Turkestan i severnyya provintsii Kitaya v g. Pekin, v 1906-7 i 8 g.g*, S.-Peterburg, 1909. (Sbornik geograficheskikh, topograficheskikh i statisticheskikh materialov po Azii, 81). This version also omitted references to Mannerheim being taken for a Swede in southern Sinkiang and all the appendices and addenda with the exception of the general map of his route. It added some acknowledgments to Russians who helped him in Urumchi and Peking, and more important, a new section on the campaign against the use of opium (pp. 145-51).

20. Mannerheim presented a copy to Senator Otto Donner, 'with respect and friendship'. This copy is now in Helsinki University Library.

21. Donner, *Sotamarsalkka vapaaherra Mannerheim*, p. 27–8. Donner, son of the senator, quoted several passages from Mannerheim's diary and from a letter to Senator Otto Donner of 7 January, 1907. Borenius, who used Donner's biography extensively, said that from Osh to Kashgar 'Gustaf Mannerheim was accompanied by M. Paul Pelliot'. *Field-Marshal Mannerheim*, p. 40. This suggested a quite different relationship from that which actually prevailed between them.

22. Omissions from the diary occur, e.g., under the entries for 18 and 30 July and 26 September, 1906.

23. Unlikely in the light of his unwillingness to appear to stress his endurance. *Cf.* note 24 below.

24. Kaarlo Hildén, 'Suomen marsalkka Mannerheimin Aasia-teoksen valmistusvaiheita; muutamia muistelmia', *Suomalais-ugrilaisen seuran aikakauskirja*, 55, v, Helsinki, 1951, p. 5.

25. Hildén, 'Suomen marsalkka Mannerheimin Aasia-teoksen valmistusvaiheita', pp. 4, 5.

26. The notebooks, manuscripts of the published versions, and photographic plates, are kept together in an old trunk, which has Kaarlo Hildén's name scrawled roughly on the lid. The first volume of the diary is signed and dated Helsingfors 1906, but bears the stamp 'Kh. K. Krikh i Ko . . . S.P.B.', and the other notebooks were probably also bought in St. Petersburg.

27. Hildén, 'Suomen marsalkka Mannerheimin Aasia-teoksen valmistusvaiheita,' p. 3.

28. Mannerheim, *Across Asia*, i, p. 509. In the original he described diary-writing as a '*corvée*'.

29. Mannerheim, *Across Asia*, i, p. 289.

30. Jägerskiöld, *Gustaf Mannerheim*, p. 63.

31. Mannerheim, *Across Asia*, i, p. 269.

32. Mannerheim, *Across Asia*, i, p. 719.

33. Mannerheim, *Across Asia*, i, p. 214.

34. Mannerheim, *Predvaritel'nyy otchet*, p. 88.

35. Mannerheim, *Across Asia*, i, p. 242.

36. Mannerheim, *Across Asia*, i, p. 436. The words 'while mounted' do not appear in the original and were presumably added 'to make the account more lively'.

37. Niiniluoto, *Suuri rooli*, p. 41.

38. Jägerskiöld, *Gustaf Mannerheim*, p. 110, quotes a letter of Mannerheim to his sister Sophie giving the length of the report as 198 pages. This discrepancy might be accounted for by the omission from the Langhoff copy of the section on the anti-opium measures included in the printed version (see above, note 19). The pages of the Langhoff copy are numbered consecutively and no omission is apparent, but a later version may have included the additional pages.

39. Mannerheim, *Predvaritel'nyy otchet*, p. 191.

40. Mannerheim, *Predvaritel'nyy otchet*, p. 188.

41. Mannerheim, *Predvaritel'nyy otchet*, p. 22.

42. Mannerheim, *Predvaritel'nyy otchet*, p. 190.

43. Mannerheim, *Predvaritel'nyy otchet*, p. 101.

44. Mannerheim, *Across Asia*, i, p. 75.

45. Mannerheim, *Predvaritel'nyy otchet*, p. 135.

46. Mannerheim, *Predvaritel'nyy otchet*, pp. 154–5.

47. Mannerheim, *Predvaritel'nyy otchet*, p. 136.

48. Mannerheim, *Predvaritel'nyy otchet*, p. 145.

49. Mannerheim, *Predvaritel'nyy otchet*, pp. 7–8.

50. Mannerheim, *Across Asia*, ii, A. K. Merisuo, 'C. G. Mannerheim's mapping work on his journey across Asia in 1906–1908', p. 6.

51. Mannerheim, *Across Asia*, i, p. 476.

52. Mannerheim, *Across Asia*, ii, Runar Meinander, 'Meteorological notes made by C. G. Mannerheim during his travels in Central Asia in 1906–1908', pp. 4, 6.

53. See above, note 15.

54. Donner, *Sotamarsalkka vapaaherra Mannerheim*, p. 77.

55. Mannerheim, *Across Asia*, i, p. 249.

56. Mannerheim, *Memoirs*, p. 72.

57. Sven Hedin, 'C. G. Mannerheim; Resa genom Asien', *Ymer; tidskrift utgiven av Svenska sällskapet för antropologi och geografi*, 60, Stockholm, 1940, p. 167. Hedin did not follow the Emperor's advice.

58. Jägerskiöld, *Gustaf Mannerheim*, p. 103.

59. See above, note 19.

60. See above, note 15.

61. Mannerheim, 'A visit to the Sarö and Shera Yögurs', p. 1.

62. *Petermanns Mitteilungen*, 55, Gotha, 1909, p. 144.

63. Mannerheim, *Across Asia*, i, p. 4.

64. Kaarlo Hildén, 'Voyage du Maréchal Mannerheim à travers l'Asie 1906–1908', *Le nord: revue internationale des pays du nord*, 4, Copenhague, 1941, p. 258.

65. See, for example, Hildén's contributions to *Festschriften* published in 1937, 1942 and 1951, and his articles in *Nordisk tidskrift* (1941), *Nouvelle revue de Hongrie* (1942), and *Suomen vapaussota* (1942). See also Sven Hedin's contribution to the 75th birthday *Festschrift* in 1942, and articles by I. Leiviskä (*Asemies*, 1942), G. J. Ramstedt (*Valvoja*, 1951), and Kustaa Vilkuna (*Hakkapeliitta*, 1932).

66. Sven Hedin, 'C. G. Mannerheims Reise durch Asien', *Petermanns geographische Mitteilungen*, 87, Gotha, 1941, p. 25.

CHAPTER IV

LAST YEARS IN RUSSIA 1908

Mannerheim went to see his relatives in Helsinki on 16–17 October, 1908, during the interval between returning to St. Petersburg and obtaining his audience with the Emperor. He was able to fit in a longer visit to Finland and Sweden while waiting for his regimental appointment after completing his report. The political situation in Finland was far less satisfactory than when he had left on his expedition. The results of the March 1907 elections, the first after the reform of parliament, had caused considerable surprise since the Social Democrats emerged as the largest party. They derived support from a substantial share of the rural vote as well as from the urban proletariat resulting from the recent industrialisation. Their programme was opposed by the conservative elements in the bourgeois parties which tended to unite on social matters, although they were divided over their willingness to co-operate with Russia and over the question of the relative status of the Finnish and Swedish languages. But parliamentary government had no chance to develop despite the creation of democratic institutions. Nor was it possible to initiate social and economic reforms. The attitude of the Emperor remained decisive. He appointed members of the Senate (the government) and approved or rejected legislation. Once the Russian government had recovered from the shock of revolution, and reaction had begun, there were ample opportunities for intervention in Finnish affairs: the constitutional freedom of Finland proved short-lived. Renewed Russian political pressure was responsible for the resignation of Mechelin in 1908. In the spring of 1909 1909 the constitutionalists left the government and the Old Finns resigned in the autumn. There seemed no prospect that the Russian government would adopt a conciliatory attitude towards Finland and Finno-Russian relations were fraught with more difficulties than ever before.

Mannerheim wanted to learn about conditions in Finland in case there should be a chance to mention the country at his audience with the

Emperor. His brother Carl had suggested he talked to Jonas Castrén and Heikki Renvall, men prominent in the struggle for Finland's constitutional rights. He contacted Renvall, arranged to meet him and Castrén, and listened to their views.[1] There is, however, no intimation that Finland was mentioned during the audience. His anxiety to be well informed about Finnish conditions revealed not only a concern for his country but also an interest in political and social affairs, a natural outcome of an upbringing in a politically conscious environment. Such political consciousness was rare among the Russian officer corps, which formed an isolated group in society, content with its apolitical role. 'Failing to understand the deep social unrest existing in the country, (the officers) remained indifferent to it or were repelled by it.'[2] Indifference to social and political questions was the antithesis of Mannerheim's outlook, which was rooted in a strong belief in the responsibility of the individual in matters of politics. The contrast was noticed not only by Mannerheim but also by some of his Russian colleagues. De Witt, for example, recalled a private conversation with him during the First World War during which he had spoken, without giving his opinion, of the difference between a single- and two-chamber parliament. This question interested him very much and de Witt stressed that there were not at that time many soldiers able to think of such details.

Nevertheless, Mannerheim was not – as yet – an active participant in politics; although he had sat in the Estate of Nobles in 1906 he had remained a silent backbencher. The intrigues of party politics were completely unattractive to him and he wrote to his sister Sophie in 1914 about the drawback of 'going sour in the acrimony which discussing politics always spreads'.[3] As his comments on the constitutional changes of 1906 showed, he was a cautious reformer. He feared the standard of parliament would be lowered and its authority diminished by the influx of inexperienced and less moderate men under the new electoral system. But although he saw the disadvantages and dangers of democracy, he recognised the need for economic and social reforms, both in Russia and Finland, and his regard for individual liberty and preference for a constitutional form of government separated him from the Russian reactionaries whose increasing influence he viewed with alarm. He considered the presence of so many troops at the opening of the First Duma made the occasion look more like the suppression of a riot than the conferment of a constitution. It was an early sign that the autocracy was recovering from the blow it had received in 1905.

Mannerheim had enjoyed his visit to his relatives in Finland and Sweden. In spite of their early separation, he and his brothers and sisters had remained in close and affectionate touch with each other. One had died as a child. Anna, the youngest girl, known as Annicka, had been sent to the Smolny Institute, a boarding school in St. Petersburg for daughters of the nobility: she died there from typhus in 1886, to the great sorrow of the family. After completing their education, the others, with the exception of Gustaf, settled in Finland until the events of the years of oppression served to disperse them once more. Carl did not return to Finland after spending his exile in Sweden. His health weakened and he died in 1915. Although he had disapproved strongly of his brother serving in the Russo-Japanese War, the trust that existed between them had never been broken. Johan also settled in Sweden, his wife's homeland, when he appeared to be in danger of persecution by the Russian authorities. He became a successful industrialist and landowner, and Mannerheim spent many happy visits at his home. Like Carl, Johan became a Swedish subject. August, the youngest in the family, died in Sweden in 1910. He had become an engineer and worked several years in South Africa. Eva married the Swedish artist Count Louis Sparre and they moved to Sweden in the summer of 1908 after living some time in Porvoo.

In 1903 Wilhelmina Mannerheim – Count Carl Robert's unmarried sister – sold Louhisaari to a stranger, without consulting the family, and moved to Sweden. The estate had belonged to the Mannerheims since 1796 and its sale was felt as a considerable loss by those who had happy memories of their childhood there. Death brought other losses. Louise von Julin, whose financial support had enabled Mannerheim to become an officer in Russia, had died in 1890. The children's affectionate grandmother, Countess Eva Mannerheim, died in 1895, and Uncle Albert in 1906. Mannerheim was to feel the sad effects of the diminution of the family circle increasingly with the passage of time, deprived as he was of the companionship he might have had from wife and children. His daughters were sent by their mother to a succession of boarding schools and his letters to them were not always answered, much to his concern. Weary of boarding school life, they eventually decided to renew contact with their father and his relatives and came to Finland: their decision was to present the family with a considerable problem.

Only Mannerheim's father and eldest sister Sophie settled permanently in Finland, and both had spent periods abroad. Count Mannerheim had remarried in Paris in 1883. His bride – and former mistress – was Baroness

Sofia Nordenstam. Their eventual return to Helsinki created an awkward situation for the Mannerheim children since their mother's relatives regarded their father with understandable distaste. However, the children managed to establish good relations with their father without upsetting their close and affectionate connections with the von Julin family. Count Carl Robert's hard work in building up a successful business after his return to Finland won him the respect of his children. Any resentment Mannerheim may have felt at the desertion of the family by his father seems to have been quickly forgotten and their warm and heartfelt relationship continued right up to the old man's death in 1914, shortly after that of his second wife. Much of his father's great charm, and a little of his recklessness, too, was reproduced in his own character, together with a good measure of his mother's energy and purposefulness. His father had a daughter, Marguerite, known as Kissi, by his second marriage. She married Michael Gripenberg in 1908 and Mannerheim got on well with both of them. He was extremely close to his sister Sophie. Her marriage to Hjalmar Linder, a friend of his, had ended in divorce, and she had then decided to take up nursing. She trained at St. Thomas's Hospital in London and returned to devote her life to the organisation of the Finnish nursing service. In 1904 she became matron of the Surgical Hospital in Helsinki. She was one of the very few people in whom he was able to confide.

Much has been written about Mannerheim's remoteness and separation from other people.[4] These characteristics were, in part at least, the consequence of his conception of how the high offices he held in Finland should be filled, and in part, too, the consequence of advancing age. He felt that loneliness increased and happiness diminished after the age of sixty as friends and relations died and staying with young people became no longer the same.[5] But his independent character did not make it easy for him to make intimate friends from among his numerous acquaintances. He generally kept his deepest feelings to himself and distrusted displays of emotion. The frankness with which he wrote to his relatives about the despair he felt during the troubled months of 1904 was exceptional. He disliked living in too close proximity to other people, complaining to his sister Sophie not long after the outbreak of war in 1914 that he was scarcely ever alone and was 'compelled day and night to live in the greatest intimacy with companions in arms whom one does not choose oneself, and whose way of looking at things is often very different from one's own'.[6] But in the atmosphere of a peace-time officers' mess in

Warsaw Mannerheim was able to relax, to cease to be commanding officer and become simply a senior colleague, an interesting conversationalist who was always ready for a joke. His charm and affable personality made him sought after as a companion. He made life-long friendships in Russia and Poland. It would be untrue to describe him as remote and isolated from other people during his service in the imperial army, especially during the years between the Asian expedition and the outbreak of the First World War which constituted one of the happiest periods of his life.

Failure to enter the School of Pages had denied him the possibility of easy success in Russia. Expulsion from the Corps of Cadets had deprived him of secure, if modest, career prospects in Finland. He had been forced to struggle for advancement against what must have seemed overpowering obstacles and disabilities – acute financial need, a severe conflict of loyalties occasioned by Russian policy in Finland, and finally a broken marriage. At last he began to experience good fortune and to win through to a position commensurate with his hopes.

Mannerheim had hoped to get command of the regiment in which he had first served, now redesignated the 5th Aleksandriyskiy Hussars, but his plans fell through because its commander failed to obtain another post. He had to take what came along, and learned while on holiday in Sweden that he had been appointed commander of the 13th Vladimir Uhlan Regiment of HIH Grand Duke Michael Nikolayevich. The appointment was published on 18 January, 1909.[7] His new regiment was stationed *1909* in the small town of Nowo Mińsk, about twenty-five miles east of Warsaw, and he hurried back from leave to join it. The principal disadvantage of service in Poland was the distance from Finland. Visits home could not be made so frequently, though he generally managed at least one trip to Finland a year, and his relatives were occasionally able to come to see him. But there was one great advantage compared with service in St. Petersburg: he did not have to live in the politically-charged, and to a Finn potentially dangerous, atmosphere of the capital. He and his family were thankful for that. Professionally, the appointment marked the beginning of a most successful and satisfying phase in his career. For the first time he was able to put into practice his exacting ideas on training and tactics. Remembering the lessons of the Russo-Japanese War, he emphasised marksmanship and dismounted action. He worked everyone very hard, especially the officers, but spared himself least of all. Strict but fair, he won loyalty and even popularity from a regiment that had hitherto acquired the reputation of being difficult to command, and raised it from a low level of training to a high state of efficiency. His work was rewarded in an unexpected but most pleasing way by the offer of the command of His Majesty's Life Guard Uhlan Regiment, part of the Independent Guards Cavalry Brigade in Warsaw. He was confirmed in this appointment, one of the best regimental commands in the cavalry, on 26 February, 1911. At the same time he was promoted Major-General, the rank held by commanders of guards regiments.[8]

Life in Warsaw, known with some justification as 'little Paris', was far more congenial than in isolated Nowo Mińsk. Mannerheim had made several Polish friends while in St. Petersburg and, as usual, his love of equestrian sports and shooting opened the way to wider social contacts. He became a member of the *Cercle de Chasse*, an association of sportsmen keenly interested in hunting roebuck, which was very popular among Russian officers. In the presence of Poles he was acutely conscious of his position in the army that had been used to destroy the liberty of Poland and turn it into a subject nation even more firmly held than Finland. But because he was not a Russian, the Poles felt they could receive him freely and as an equal, without any political stigma attaching to themselves. He got on very well with members of the Polish aristocracy, whose friendship he valued highly and whose generous hospitality he never forgot. He sympathised with their feelings about Russian oppression and admired the tenacity with which they preserved their culture and way of life in such difficult circumstances. Privately, he considered Russian policy in Poland immoral, corrupting, and politically unwise, and believed the Russian failure to solve the Polish question marked the failure of the unifying policy of Slav nationalism, but that Poland, like Finland, would eventually secure a freer position in a reformed Empire. Reports from the Gendarmerie criticising his friendly contacts with the Poles were disregarded by the Russian authorities as insignificant.[9] He had a powerful protector in the Governor-General, General Georg Scalon de Coligny, a member of the important family which had assisted him in the past. But his loyalty to the Emperor was never seriously doubted by Russians or Poles. The Germans were to find that he had the reputation in Warsaw of being not only ambitious and adventurous but also a Russian monarchist.[10]

As the commander of a guards regiment Mannerheim came into regular contact with the Emperor and was invited from time to time to take part in shoots at Spala, the imperial hunting lodge near Warsaw. On 18 October, 1912, the Emperor showed his appreciation of Mannerheim's services by making him a Major-General *à la suite*.[11] Officially, the Major-Generals *à la suite* formed part of Imperial General Headquarters, but their numbers varied according to the Emperor's wishes and the title was in fact a token of the sovereign's personal regard and involved no special military or court duties. It was, however, a relatively easy matter for a Major-General *à la suite* to obtain an audience, and the privilege of wearing the imperial monogram and the aiguillettes carried considerable prestige. Indeed, many preferred to remain in the rank of Major-General than to be promoted Lieutenant-General and cease to be *à la suite*. The title was in a sense the highest point of Mannerheim's Russian career and was one of which he was certainly very proud. De Witt believed that, had he not been promoted Lieutenant-General after the revolution, he would not have removed the imperial cipher from his epaulettes, a defiance that could have cost him his life. Years later when Finnish visitors to his Helsinki home expressed surprise at the presence of a picture of Nicolas II, regarded in Finland as an oppressor, he simply replied: 'He was my Emperor.'[12] Although he disapproved of his policy, he felt a liking for him as a man, and loyalty towards him as his sovereign: loyalty outweighed disapproval. He remarked in his *Memoirs* on the Emperor's simplicity and lack of ostentation in the company of his officers. [13]He was pleased to find that his sister Sophie shared his favourable impression of the Emperor when she was presented to him in Helsinki in 1915. The Emperor's favour to Mannerheim extended to the grant of a special allowance from imperial funds that was raised at the request of the Minister-Secretary of State in 1913, the Emperor speaking very flatteringly of Mannerheim and stating that it was a pleasure to increase the payment.[14]

Without doubt the imperial allowance was a very welcome addition to the moderate pay of a Major-General. His position was expensive to maintain, and he found it difficult to lay out more than 15,000 francs a year for his daughters' upbringing. First Sophy, and then Anastasie, had come to Finland in 1912 and had stayed for a time with their grandfather and Aunt Sophie. Mannerheim felt it would be undesirable for them to join him in Warsaw as the international situation was so uncertain – an argument that has the sound of an excuse – and was deeply grateful for the help he received in looking after them. Anastasie had been converted to Roman Catholicism and was determined to become a nun. Her aunt's efforts to interest her in nursing failed and she entered a Carmelite convent in London in 1914. Her father respected her decision though he felt sad about it. He was closer to his mother's religious feeling than to his father's indifference.[15] At the end of 1914 Sophy managed to return to Finland via Sweden from Switzerland where she had been staying with the wife of one of Mannerheim's brother-officers when the First World War began. In 1917 she, too, went to London, under her aunt's influence, to take up nursing; this was gratifying news to her father. As usual, the family had rallied round to help him, this time to try to solve the problems of where his daughters were to live and what they were to do.

Mannerheim's elevation to the suite of His Majesty made him one of the most senior Finns in the imperial army. As such he came under consideration for recommendation to the Emperor for the important post of Minister-Secretary of State when the request to resign of its then holder, Baron August Langhoff, was reconsidered in the autumn of 1912. The Office of the Secretary of State for Finland was established in St. Petersburg for the conduct of business requiring the decision of the Emperor-Grand Duke. The function of the Minister-Secretary of State, its head, was to report to the Emperor all matters, except such as were purely military, submitted for His Majesty's consideration by the Senate and the Governor-General. He was also the intermediary agent for correspondence with the ministers and other higher authorities of the Empire on matters relating both to the Empire and to Finland. He countersigned imperial rescripts and communicated other imperial decisions to the Governor-General.[16]

It was felt by some prominent Finns that Mannerheim had many personal qualifications for this post in addition to being well regarded by the Emperor and possessing useful connections with leading circles in Russia. Langhoff probably mentioned the matter to Mannerheim and favoured his candidature.[17] The prospect was initially attractive, offering the chance to work for the reconciliation of Finland and Russia, and he is said to have discussed the question with Finnish politicians. However, the realisation that there was at that time no hope of moderating Russian policy towards Finland led him to decide against allowing his name to go forward. The intensive measures of russification during the three preceding years indicated the extremes to which the Russian government was prepared to go in its determination to destroy Finnish autonomy. Russians were appointed members of the Senate and to posts in the civil service. In June 1910 the Duma passed a law removing 'matters of imperial concern' from the competence of the Finnish parliament, reducing it to the level of a provincial consultative assembly. Finally, in January 1912, the Duma enacted that Russian subjects in Finland should possess the same rights there as Finnish citizens. It was hardly a favourable climate for reconciliation.

At this stage it was also by no means certain that the Emperor would accept a recommendation to appoint a Finn as Minister-Secretary of State. Later, the Emperor actually stated to Langhoff that he did not personally know any Finns who would be suitable, so Mannerheim's candidature could hardly have succeeded: Lieutenant-General Vladimir Ivanovich Markov, who replaced Langhoff in April 1913, though a Finnish subject, was more Russian than Finnish.[18] Mannerheim was in fact fortunate to avoid a post in which a severe conflict of loyalties would have been inevitable. Significantly, there is no mention of the episode in his *Memoirs*, which are generally silent on the 'ifs' of his life, and which in any case have little to say about his views on Finno-Russian relations during this period, perhaps because they were at variance with the Finnish constitutionalist attitude accepted after independence as the normal patriotic line. Nevertheless, his consideration for nomination by certain influential Finns, including the well-known constitutionalist Emil Schybergson, who belonged to the Swedish Party, showed that his qualities were recognised to some extent in Finland, and also that his political outlook, of which his continued service in Russia throughout both periods of oppression must have been regarded as a reflection, was not considered an obstacle to his appointment; indeed, it could have been a basis for it.[19]

As commander of His Majesty's Life Guard Uhlans, Mannerheim enhanced his reputation as a very able soldier. He mentioned in his *Memoirs* that the Inspector of Cavalry complimented him highly on the training of the regiment.[20] This standard was attained by demanding but considerate leadership. One of his subordinates and future Chief of Staff, Prince Leonid Jeletski, wrote of the skill with which he led the life of the regiment and the intensity with which he prepared it for war.[21] He knew the practical value of equestrian sports in creating fit, strong riders, and encouraged his officers to develop their skill as horsemen by entering keenly into sporting activities himself. By carefully arranged postings he even managed to remove some of the older colonels and squadron commanders and appoint younger and more vigorous men in their places. Ceremonial occasions punctuated the routine of training. In 1909 he had

the honour of leading a cavalry contingent at the parade held to commemorate the two hundredth anniversary of the decisive Swedish defeat
at Poltava, a strange irony of which his family was very conscious. In
1912 he was present at the celebration of the centenary of the battle of
Borodino and also at the unveiling of the monument to Alexander III
in Moscow. The following autumn he visited the French cavalry school
at Saumur.

Militarily, as well as socially, these years were exceptionally happy and
he did not look forward to the prospect of leaving Warsaw to take up a
brigade command elsewhere. In 1913 he rejected the offer of command
of a Cuirassier Brigade at Tsarskoye Selo, preferring to wait for a vacancy
in the Independent Guards Cavalry Brigade in Warsaw, of which he had
been acting commander on several occasions. He must have sensed the
favourable attitude of the authorities towards him to run the risk of
rejecting an appointment. However, his confidence was justified and on
6 January, 1914, he obtained the much-sought post of commander of the
Independent Guards Cavalry Brigade.[22] This formation comprised the
Grodno Hussars of the Guard, a battery of horse artillery, and his own
Uhlan regiment, of which he remained a member. As he stated in a proud
farewell order of the day to them, he was happy to remain an Uhlan of
His Majesty 'to the very grave'.[23]

Pleasure at the appointment was marred by concern about his health.
His 'Manchurian' rheumatism had become so bad that he feared he might
have to retire from the army. He had visited health resorts in Germany in
previous years and, before taking such a drastic step, decided to try a cure
at Wiesbaden in the summer of 1914. It had some beneficial effects. In
any case, the international situation soon banished thoughts of retirement.
He could feel tension rising in Germany, as in the rest of Europe, following the assassination at Sarajevo on 28 June of the Archduke Francis
Ferdinand of Austria. The drift towards war had begun. On 22 July he
was back in Warsaw. The Austro-Hungarian ultimatum to Serbia was
delivered the next day.

From his observations in Germany, and from the way events were
moving, he felt certain that war was imminent. His brigade was on
manoeuvres when he rejoined them and he was unlucky enough to be
thrown from his horse when leading a charge, hurting his foot. Although
the injury turned out to be only a sprain, he found the hindrance to his
mobility particularly annoying at such a time. It did not stop him from
making his personal preparations for a campaign, going through the bags

he kept packed ready for manoeuvres, and having a short haircut. The brigade had been ordered back to Warsaw and it was there on 29 July that he received the order to mobilise. Austria had mobilised against Serbia the previous day and, in turn, Russia ordered partial mobilisation on the Austrian frontier. Cavalry formations in Poland were always at a high state of readiness and mobilisation was rapid: Mannerheim's brigade left Warsaw six hours after being told to mobilise. He travelled by car to Lublin, where his brigade detrained on 30 July, and marched twenty-five miles to Kraśnik near the frontier with Galicia. Full Russian, Austrian, French and German mobilisation followed by 1 August, when Germany declared war on France. The Austro-Hungarian declaration of war on Russia did not follow until 6 August.

Russian war plans envisaged operations both south and north of the Polish salient. In the south the aim was to envelop the Austrians north of the Carpathians, seize Galicia and secure the passes into Hungary; in the north to envelop East Prussia. The latter offensive, mounted in mid-August, was completely defeated by mid-September and offset the success of the actions against the Austrians, whose advance from north-east Galicia into Poland was driven back. Mannerheim's brigade formed part of a cavalry corps commanded by Lieutenant-General Prince Tumanov covering the deployment of the Fourth Army. Early on 17 August elements of the advance guard of the Austrian First Army began to move against the position of the Russian cavalry at Kraśnik. Tumanov ordered Mannerheim south to stop the enemy advance at any cost. His whole brigade, together with two *sotnias* (squadrons) of Frontier Guards, was soon heavily engaged against superior forces on a five-mile front. He tried to use the 13th Vladimir Uhlans, who were put under his command, to attack the enemy in the rear. Austrian attempts to envelop the Russian right caused him concern, but he received invaluable support from an artillery battery that Tumanov had ordered forward to help him, and infantry were hurrying towards the battle; the 6th Regiment of Rifles foiled the enveloping movement, and towards evening the Independent Guards Cavalry Brigade was relieved by the 69th Infantry Regiment. The Austrians retreated in confusion and lost a considerable number of prisoners. Mannerheim's own casualties were heavy, especially in the Life Guard Uhlans; it had, however, been a joy to see them under fire. In holding up the enemy advance for six hours by dismounted action his regiments had proved their worth, and he recognised the great importance for morale of the successful nature of their first engagement.

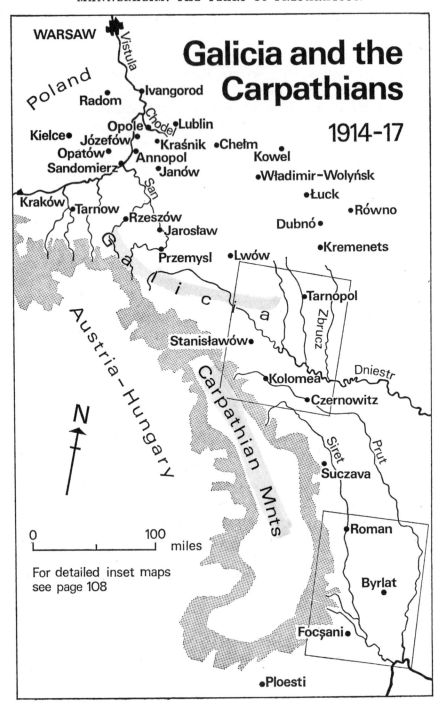

Galicia and the Carpathians 1914-17

For detailed inset maps see page 108

Jeletski, Chief of Staff of the brigade, considered that Mannerheim's complete fearlessness and contempt of death contributed to a great extent to that success. 'His tall, impressive figure turned up in all parts of the position. Smoking his cigar, he appeared in particular at places where the situation was becoming critical.' Tumanov recommended him for the Cross of St. George, the premier Russian decoration for conspicuous gallantry or distinguished service in battle, but he had to wait a little longer for this honour. But eventually the award of the Sword of St. George was to show recognition of his own part in the battle, which by disrupting Austrian plans won for the Russians a six-day respite during which they completed their own deployment.[24]

The Russian Fourth and Austrian First Armies went over to the offensive almost simultaneously, and on 23 August a second battle of Kraśnik began which formed an introduction to a general battle in the Lublin-Lwów region. Tumanov's cavalry, the 13th Cavalry Division with the Independent Guards Cavalry Brigade, on the right of the Fourth Army, was ordered to operate on the flank and rear of the enemy, but their attempts to advance towards Annopol were defeated by the attacking Austrians. The Russians were forced back from Kraśnik in the direction of Lublin and the Austrian enveloping movement threatened the vital railway between Lublin and Ivangorod (Deblin). Between 25 and 27 August Tumanov reported Austrian units advancing towards Opole and the situation became more serious during the night of 28/29 August when an Austrian corps crossed the Vistula at Józefów, moving on Opole towards the Chodel. Tumanov was ordered to halt this advance.

Already on 28 August he had reinforced Mannerheim's brigade with two regiments and ordered him to find out the strength of the enemy approaching Opole and prevent them from crossing the river. Mannerheim encountered strong opposition just south of Opole, but his attempt to turn the right flank of the enemy forces there was nullified by the enveloping movement of their left and he was told to withdraw across the Chodel. The 13th Cavalry Division was unable to hold the river crossings, and early on 29 August the Austrians had seized four bridgeheads on the north bank of the river, but Mannerheim's brigade, reinforced with another regiment, recaptured the crossings and held them during the night. The following day he handed over their defence to the newly-arrived 23rd Infantry Division and, to support the division's advance southwards, his brigade, with two additional regiments under command, made a deep turning movement along bad forest roads in boggy country towards Opole. The appearance of his troops there turned the renewed Austrian attack across the Chodel into a sudden retreat to the south-east. Such bold flanking movements, which made full use of the mobility and flexibility of the cavalry arm, were typical of Mannerheim's tactics and application of the principle of offensive action. In this case the outcome was spectacular, and Tumanov rightly attributed to Mannerheim the whole honour for the success of the action.[25]

By 3 September the battle of Lublin-Lwów had entered its last phase as the Russian south-western armies went over to the offensive; victory had been clearly won by 9 September. During this stage of the battle Mannerheim's brigade was attached to the Corps of the Guard and took part in the operations towards the river San and beyond it, which went on until 25 September. At Janów his brigade captured an army supply train of over 2,000 waggons. The Russian offensive had been successful all along the south-western front: Lwów and Jarosław were captured, Przemyśl invested, and the Bukovina overrun. The Austrians had to retreat to the Wisłoka and their losses of men, as well as of territory, had been severe.

Russian losses, too, were considerable. Major-General Sir Alfred Knox, the British military attaché in St. Petersburg who became a liaison officer at the front after the outbreak of war, recorded an interesting conversation in September 1914 with two ladies dressed in black. 'They told me of the death of young Bibikov, who belonged to the Lancers of Warsaw and was killed in a charge by the Independent Guard Cavalry Brigade against infantry in a wood. Mannerheim, his General, kissed the dead boy and said he would like to be in his place. Mannerheim is blamed for squandering lives. Poor Bibikov won all the prizes at the Concours Hippique at Vienna three years ago . . .'[26] Rodzyanko, who was attached to Knox from time to time, described Mannerheim as 'heartbroken' at Bibikov's death.[27] Jeletski's account of the incident reveals that Mannerheim's reaction was undoubtedly due largely to his personal responsibility for the death of one of his favourite officers. He had asked Bibikov why he had not advanced against the enemy and had been told there were only fourteen men left in his squadron. Taunted by Mannerheim's thoughtless question, 'Are you afraid?' Bibikov led his men forward and fell almost at once.[28]

This regrettable episode helped to quell Mannerheim's reckless bravery. Princess Marie Lubomirska, with whom he had a diligent and intimate correspondence during the early part of the war, wrote in her diary:

'People say that Mannerheim is extraordinarily brave but that he leads his troops to a certain death.'[29] The same could have been said of many cavalry commanders, raised in the tradition of self-sacrifice expected of cavalry in war. Soon, however, Mannerheim was expressing ever-increasing concern at the wastage of life and the high price of military success. All bravado was to be condemned. He wondered whether the objectives gained were sufficiently important to justify the sacrifices involved. He was conscious of the appalling consequences of war for the civilian population of the areas fought over. German brutality, robbery and destruction shocked him, and he hoped Warsaw would escape occupation. It pleased him when Russian troops were well received by the inhabitants of areas previously occupied by the enemy, but the Russian scorched earth policy in retreat was to make him ashamed and disgusted. War made him a more serious man, determined to keep casualties and destruction to a minimum, though not to the extent that the fear of losses deterred him from a necessary course of action.

The effect of the scale of the war on the army as a whole was before long apparent. Wastage proved far higher than had been anticipated, especially among regular officers and NCOs, and soon drafts were being sent to the front only partially trained. Russia was ill-prepared for a long war. Industry and communications proved unequal to the sudden demands placed on them. An acute shortage of shells was to hamper operations and cause morale to fall. The army and the mass of the people had their confidence shaken in the leadership of the nation as the few early successes were followed by unrelieved disasters, and skilful propaganda organised by the government's political opponents exploited the situation.

Austria requested help from the Germans and on 28 September Hindenburg began to advance from Silesia towards Warsaw on a broad front between Kraków and Częstochowa, the immediate objectives of his right wing being Opatów and Sandomierz. At first there was little opposition since the Russians had denuded the area of troops to strengthen the shoulders of the Polish salient. But their Commander-in-Chief, Grand Duke Nikolas Nicolayevich, had decided to regroup his armies for a counter-offensive by moving twelve corps from Galicia to the middle Vistula around Ivangorod, while at the same time falling back across the San. On 1 October the Ninth Army formed a detachment under General Delsal, composed of two brigades of rifles and the Independent Guards Cavalry Brigade, to cover the bridges of Annopol and Zawichost during the extensive troop movements across the San.

Although muddy roads impeded all movement, Mannerheim took up his position covering the road from Opatów to Sandomierz on 2 October. The rifles were west and south of Opatów, with Mannerheim some distance to their left; his squadrons dismounted on a front of four miles and his advanced detachments became engaged that day. The action became general on 3 October but he managed to hold on to his position at Klimontów until the arrival of the 319th Infantry Regiment enabled him to pull back slightly. On 4 October a heavy enemy attack on Opatów, accompanied by a circling movement north of the town, caused General Delsal to begin to withdraw on Sandomierz. Without warning, the 5th Cavalry Division, which had held the sector between Mannerheim and the rifles, abandoned its position. This imperilled the rifles' line of retreat and made it impossible for Mannerheim to carry out Delsal's order to cover the area north-west of Opatów. Taking matters into his own hands, Mannerheim decided to stay where he was, and by his energetic defence made possible the extrication of the rifles. He received orders to withdraw to Sandomierz that night. At a cost of 7,000 casualties, the action of General Delsal's detachment had held up Hindenburg's offensive for three days and made it possible for other units of the Ninth Army to recross to the right bank of the San with their baggage and heavy artillery.[30] For his own part in the battle, Mannerheim was awarded the 4th class of the Order of St. George. The telegram informing him of the award arrived during the night and Jeletski, who described the incident, had difficulty in waking him. The news obviously gave him intense pleasure and he expressed his feelings – in itself a rare occurrence – by saying aloud several times, 'How I am pleased'. He telegraphed his sister Sophie and in a subsequent letter remarked that he could now die peacefully; to do so before getting the little white cross of the Order of St. George would have worried him, if not here, then surely in another world.[31]

The battle of Opatów-Klimontów began a series of battles on the left bank of the Vistula from Ivangorod to Warsaw, and by 12 October the Germans were within seven miles of the Polish capital. But the Russian concentration and the absence of reinforcements compelled them to withdraw. By 27 October the Germans began a general retreat, devastating communications and thus greatly impeding the Russian advance, which managed nevertheless to clear most of Russian Poland by the end of the month. The Austrian advance in Galicia had failed by 9 October to do more than take Jarosław and relieve Przemyśl, and by mid-October the Austrians, too, had begun to retreat. Hindenburg began a new offensive in north Poland in the middle of November. There was bitter fighting around Łódź, which fell on 6 December, and the Russians withdrew to the lines of the rivers Rawka and Bzura west of Warsaw.

During this period the Independent Guards Cavalry Brigade was attached to the Corps of the Guard and justified the high regard of General Bezobrazov, the corps commander, who refused to split it up among his infantry divisions although he had no divisional cavalry and thus had difficulty in keeping contact with the enemy. Mannerheim fought at Ivangorod in mid-October, and later took part in the offensive against the Austrians, penetrating as far as the fortifications around Kraków by the end of November. However, an Austrian counter-offensive soon pushed the Russians back from Kraków to the Dunajec. Mannerheim spent Christmas near Kielce. At the end of January 1915 a German–Austrian offensive in the Carpathians necessitated extensive regrouping of the Russian forces, and in February the Independent Guards Cavalry Brigade was sent to join the Eighth Army in Galicia. Mannerheim seized this opportunity to go to Warsaw to pack up and store his home there.

He rejoined his brigade near Lwów and rode on towards Sambor, where General Brusilov, the army commander – his former chief at the Officers' Cavalry School – had his headquarters. Brusilov inspected the brigade and asked Mannerheim if he had any special wishes. There had been rumours that the Independent Guards Cavalry Brigade was to be reformed as a division, and Mannerheim asked Brusilov if he could remain with it, were the rumours true. Brusilov agreed, in so far as the decision should lie with him, but that evening sent Mannerheim a telegram offering him the command of the 12th Cavalry Division. He was reluctant to leave his brigade and hesitated, but Brusilov made it clear at an interview he requested that such an offer was not to be refused. He left at once on 3 March for Stanisławów, ninety miles to the south-east, where his division was in action.

The suddenness of Mannerheim's transfer had been caused by General Aleksey Maksimovich Kaledin, the division's highly successful commander, becoming a casualty. Kaledin recovered and went on to command a corps and an army, though without distinction, but until he received a new post Mannerheim was officially only acting commander of the 12th Cavalry Division. His appointment, which reflected Brusilov's confidence in him and the reputation he had acquired with the Independent Guards Cavalry Brigade, was confirmed on 7 July, 1915.[32] Sad though he was to leave his brigade, Mannerheim appreciated the quality of the division, which he described to his sister as first-rate. He perceived the devotion of the staff to Kaledin and was careful to leave all appointments unchanged. In September, however, he received a new chief of staff, Colonel Mikhail Mikhailovich Georgievich, with whom he got on less well than he had with Jeletski, but whose work he valued. Of the four cavalry regiments in the division,[33] the 12th Akhtyrskiy Hussars, which dated back to the mid-seventeenth century and had the Grand Duchess Olga Aleksandrovna as their Colonel-in-Chief, aroused his special admiration. The division was recruited mainly from Ukrainian peasants. Together with the so-called Wild Division, a poorly-trained and unreliable formation of Caucasian volunteers commanded by the Grand Duke Michael Aleksandrovich, it formed part of General Khan Nakhichevanskiy's IInd Cavalry Corps.

The devotion to his predecessor, which Mannerheim had noticed at once at headquarters, extended throughout the division and he was not looked on favourably at first. S. de Witt observed him closely when he came to dine with the 12th Bielgorodskiy Uhlans. 'My impressions: a man who compelled attention, very tall, very handsome and very cold. It was rare that he said "no", or that he did not agree, but he would turn his head away a little, bend it back and cast a calm, scornful glance into space. The conversation was always cut short. In addition, he had a terrible Swedish accent. From time to time his knowledge of the Russian language was deficient. First impression unfavourable.' De Witt's squadron commander commented: 'We shall see later on; at the moment it is not a tremendous beginning – it is not the same thing as General Kaledin.'

After hard fighting in the region of Stanisławów while the Russians were attempting to hold up the enemy between the Prut and the Dniestr until a new line could be formed along the latter river, the 12th Cavalry Division was pulled back across the Dniestr and ordered thirty miles east to Zaleszczyki to prevent the enemy from crossing the river there. The 9th Army, under which Mannerheim now came, was conducting an aggressive defence to stop the enemy transferring troops to another sector, and for a while at the end of March the 12th Cavalry Division held part of an exposed bridgehead south of the Dniestr. They were then moved another fifteen miles eastwards to Uście Biskupie where Mannerheim recrossed the river on 2 April and established a bridgehead during the next two days. But his success was not exploited, his supporting infantry failed to withstand a counter-attack, and he had to withdraw, releasing the Austrians from a critical situation.[34] From then until May his task was the defence of a sector on the south bank of the Dniestr. General

Khan Nakhichevanskiy had been wounded at Zaleszczki and Mannerheim acted for a while as corps commander, impatient all the time to return to his division, where he felt more at home than in a merely temporary position of great responsibility.

The Austrians had made some progress in Galicia in February when they had taken Czernowitz and Stanisławów, but they had soon lost the latter place and the Russians recovered ground in the mountains. But the military situation of the Russians worsened appreciably as 1915 went on. Early in May a powerful German offensive at Gorlice smashed the whole Russian front in Galicia and by the end of June that province had been cleared of the Russians. In July the Germans began two offensives, advancing from Galicia towards Lublin and Chełm, and southwards towards Warsaw, which fell on 5 August. By the end of the month the Russians had lost Brest-Litovsk, 125 miles further east, and a resumption of fighting in September caused the loss of Łuck. The front now ran south-east from Riga to Dvinsk, and then roughly south through Baranowicze and Dubnó to Tarnopol and Czernowitz.

Mannerheim's troops were heavily engaged throughout the summer. The 9th Army began an offensive across the Dniester in the Bukovina on 10 May in a vain attempt to relieve the pressure from the Germans attacking at Gorlice. In this operation Mannerheim acted as a corps commander, driving from Horodenka towards Kolomea. Later in May his forces were ordered east to defend the line of the Prut west of Sniatyn. Early in June his division moved to Halicz, north of Stanisławów, to cover the retreat of the XIth Corps and its passage across the Dniestr. He then covered the retreat of the XXIInd Corps over the Gnila Lipa, and later covered more troops withdrawing over the Zlota Lipa. After a week's rest early in July the 12th Cavalry Division had to return to the Zaleszczyki area, where it again came under the command of General Khan Nakhichevanskiy. The Caucasian Wild Division failed to support a promising attack Mannerheim made across the Dniestr and, as at Uście Biskupie in April, he had to withdraw. His division had a period of rest until 20 July but for the remainder of the month and throughout August it was involved in hard fighting in defence of a sector of the Dniestr and in preventing the enemy crossing the rivers Strypa and Sereth.

The rheumatism that had been so bad in the summer of 1914 had become much worse as a result of the rigours of life in the field and by August 1915 he could hardly take a step. A doctor in Kiev advised him to take a cure at the hot springs at Odessa and, although he disliked leaving his

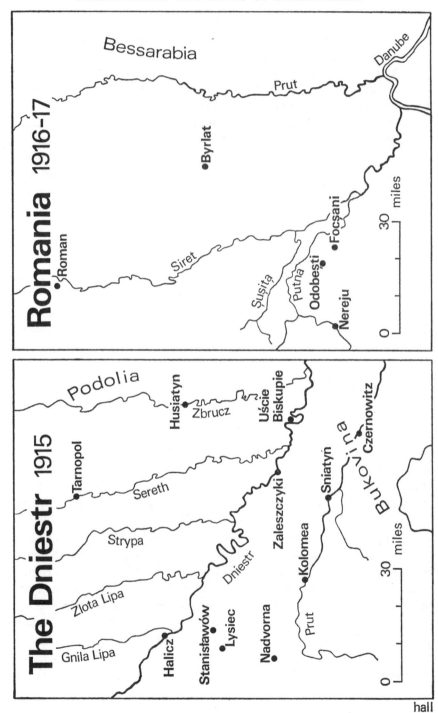

hall

troops, he handed over his command and went. The rest was enjoyable and the treatment helpful, but perhaps the best part of the stay at Odessa was the visit of his sister Sophie, who came from Helsinki to keep him company. The interlude did not last long. He was back at the front in mid-September. There was fighting during the autumn on the Dniestr and the Sereth, and at times Mannerheim again commanded the IInd Cavalry Corps. In October seven of his squadrons successfully carried out a spectacular night attack at Haiworonka, charging through three lines of enemy trenches and destroying a German infantry regiment in what he described as *'une très-jolie opération'*.[35] His division was in a defensive position north-west of Chotin from early November and not until mid-December, when the fighting on the borders of Podolia had died down, was it withdrawn to rest in the area around Husiatyn.

The 12th Cavalry Division was transferred to the 7th Army to take part in an offensive in January but never became involved in the fighting. Mannerheim took advantage of the quiet situation to visit Finland in February 1916, his first trip home since 1913. As well as his sister Sophie, his younger daughter was in Helsinki, and his brother Johan and sister-in-law came over from Sweden to see him. It was a pleasant rest, and by meeting so many friends and acquaintances in Helsinki and St. Petersburg he was able to become more familiar with political developments. His division had been sent into winter quarters near Równo, just under 40 miles east of Łuck, where it became part of the forces of the 8th Army earmarked for the summer offensive. The front remained calm throughout the spring.

The appalling losses of men and equipment in the disasters of 1915 were received in Russia with a spirit of patriotic self-sacrifice which the Emperor, who assumed the supreme command, found difficult to exploit because the liberals and the leaders of the voluntary organisations that had sprung up failed to work harmoniously with the authorities. They demanded a place in the government, and the Emperor felt bound to refuse their demand for constitutional change while the country was at war. Mannerheim criticised this decision. Determined to gain power, the liberals and progressives then began a vociferous propaganda campaign against the conduct of the war by the Emperor and the government which had the effect of demoralising the whole of society and contributed to the immediate collapse of the government on the outbreak of the March revolution in 1917.

Mannerheim regretted the dismissal of the Grand Duke Nicolas

Nikolayevich, a competent and firm commander, as a scapegoat for the failures of 1915. He knew the Emperor would be Commander-in-Chief in name only, but felt that the post would expose him unnecessarily to criticism and prevent him from paying adequate attention to non-military affairs. Nevertheless, the position of the Russian army had improved in all respects by the spring of 1916: the new reserve officers were enthusiastic even if their military knowledge was slender; industry and transport were better organised and the supply of arms and ammunition had increased. Attacks at Lake Narocz in mid-March 1916, intended to relieve the pressure on Verdun, failed completely, but plans were made for a big offensive against Vilna in the summer. The heavy Austrian attack on Italy in the middle of May brought about an appeal to Russia for help which caused changes in the timing and direction of the Russian plans. General Brusilov, in command of the South-Western Front, was eager to begin an offensive he had planned against Łuck and another in the Bukovina, and his armies struck on 4 June. He had been able to accumulate sufficient ammunition for an effective artillery bombardment that contributed to the abrupt collapse of Austrian resistance.

On the night of 4 June Mannerheim moved to Warkowiczy ready to penetrate into the enemy rear when the breakthrough was made. It came earlier than expected, and the next day he was ordered to a point north of Dubnó and succeeded during the night in making his way by forced marches through the shattered Austrian lines to begin his advance on the Styr. Although out of contact with 8th Army headquarters, he had reached Torgowica on 7 June, where he intended to ford the river, but enemy opposition was too great. He attached himself to a nearby corps, and later, on hearing that Łuck had fallen, moved north to cross the Styr there. His orders were to cut the enemy's communications with Władimir-Wolyńsk, and to do so he aimed to occupy Torczyn, a road junction west of Łuck. Austrian resistance was stiff and despite hard fighting he was unable to advance far. His men and horses were tired after five days and nights of action, and he was able to give them only half a day's rest before resuming his attack on Torczyn. But before the village fell, on 11 June, he swung west towards Zaturcy where he was able to break through the advance to within twelve miles of Władimir-Wolyńsk during the following three days.

His next task was to cover the regrouping of the Russian infantry west of Kiselin. Around Kiselin and Woronczyn he became involved in heavy fighting against the Germans who were counter-attacking from Kowel

On 17 June a charge by two *sotnias* of his Orenburg Cossacks destroyed a Württemburg infantry regiment and restored a dangerous situation near Kiselin. The German counter-attack made little progress. Despite considerable casualties during June and July, the division had fought magnificently and Mannerheim had handled it brilliantly during a series of 'first aid' actions. The Russian offensive was halted at the end of July, and the division was moved into trenches around Kiselin near the river Stochod in August, by which time the fighting had died down on that part of the front. But further south Brusilov was able to sustain his offensive until the end of September. He made excellent progress in Galicia and overran the Bukovina. He had won a victory, but it was far from decisive, and its most important indirect result, the entry of Romania into the war on the side of the Entente at the end of August, was to add to Russia's problems.

The Romanian army was badly equipped and led, and its invasion of Transylvania left the strategically important Dobruja exposed to attack. The Germans quickly took advantage of the faulty Romanian dispositions. By the end of September Mackensen had forced the Romanians back to the Danube, and Falkenhayn had compelled the invaders of Transylvania to retreat. In November the Germans forced their way through the mountains and began to advance on Bucharest, which they entered on 6 December. At first the Russians had been reluctant to intervene, despite Romanian appeals for aid, but the development of a threat to Odessa made it necessary for them to dispatch large numbers of troops to support the defeated remnant of the Romanian army. This strained considerably their resources and lengthened their front.

Mannerheim's division was among the formations ordered to Romania. It had remained in the Łuck region during the late summer of 1916 and its commander had even been able to attend a Chevalier Guards' dinner behind the Kowel front in September. In October the division was moved further south to the vicinity of Kremenets and the Pochayev Monastery, some twenty-five miles south of Dubnó, where it was put into reserve and brought up to strength in men and horses. Now, at the end of November, Mannerheim began a march of about 350 miles to his new location. The route lay through the ravaged areas of Galicia and the Bukovina, and a Cossack division was marching ahead of him along the same road. De Witt remarked that the thatch off the roofs was the only forage obtainable in the countryside. And yet Mannerheim's arrangements were so good that, while the Cossacks lost horses by the dozen, only five were lost by his division. 'From day to day regard for Mannerheim increased, as did his authority.' On 20 December Mannerheim reached Odobeşti.

Continued German pressure in the Transylvanian Alps meant that the 12th Cavalry Division had to be put into the line immediately to defend the approaches to Focşani and the valley of the Siret. He took command of a sector about thirty-eight miles long, in mountainous country crossed by the rivers Şuşiţa, Putna, Neruja and Zabala, and his force, known as Group Wrancza,[36] grew from his own division and a Romanian brigade to comprise a mixed Russian and Romanian corps of four cavalry divisions, two infantry divisions and an infantry brigade. De Witt recalled that at first Mannerheim had resorted to inviting Romanian officers to dinner to give him the chance to put Russians in their places and thus stiffen the resistance of the demoralised Romanian troops. Although the mountain conditions were strange to the Russian cavalrymen and the weather was bad, they fought well in the fierce battles of December and January that contributed to the stabilisation of the front. Mannerheim left Group Wrancza towards the end of January 1917 when the 12th Cavalry Division was withdrawn to Bessarabia to rest and receive reinforcements. There was forage in Bessarabia: none was to be found in Romania or the Bukovina.

From Bessarabia Mannerheim received permission to go to Finland for short leave. While passing through Petrograd in the middle of February he reported to the Emperor and the Empress at Tsarskoye Selo. He found the Emperor absent-minded, but the Empress unusually lively and interested in what he had to say. He learned from her of the defection to the enemy of Colonel Sturdza, a Romanian who had served under his command and whom he had regarded as an excellent officer, incapable of such a thing. Such misjudgment of character was exceptional for Mannerheim. He could not help noticing the tense atmosphere of the capital, which contrasted with the calm of Helsinki, where he met some of his old friends and former fellow-cadets, talked to them about the war and his own recent operations, and familiarised himself as best he could with conditions in the country. On returning from Helsinki to Petrograd on 9 March he encountered the outbreak of the revolution. There had been demonstrations by large numbers of strikers that day and the movement grew in intensity during 10 March. The following day government counter-measures appeared to have succeeded in overcoming the unrest but on 12 March some army units mutinied and joined the crowds; by the end of the day Petrograd had succumbed to the revolution.

Mannerheim went to the ballet on the evening of 11 March and found the streets deserted when he left the Imperial Opera – a clear indication of crisis. Next day there were revolutionary crowds of soldiers and civilians outside his hotel, the Hôtel de l'Europe on the corner of the Nevsky and the Mikhailovskaya. As he looked from the window of his room his uniform was excitedly pointed out by a demonstrator, and, warned by the hotel porter that officers were being arrested, he escaped down the service stairs to the nearby office of a friend. He was fortunate to avoid detention by a patrol that challenged him in the street and by another group that searched the house of a Finn where he took refuge. Some sort of order had returned to the city by 14 March when he was able to go back to his hotel. The following day he left on the night train for Moscow, arriving to see revolutionary demonstrations in the streets. After a couple of days there he continued his journey to the front.

The events of that week became clear only gradually. The government had underestimated the seriousness of the trouble building up in Petrograd and the counter-measures ordered by the Emperor were based on inadequate information. It was an ominous sign that his government had lost its power when soldiers refused to obey orders to fight the mutineers and strikers. The Duma had been in session when the troubles began and in effect ignored the imperial order of prorogation on 12 March. It sent emissaries to the Emperor to ask him to abdicate, and since the generals that he had consulted also advised abdication, he did so with surprising readiness on 15 March. Unlike the generals around the Emperor, some of the politicians had no desire to save the monarchy, and the Grand Duke Michael, whom the Emperor had named as his successor, was also persuaded to abdicate. On 16 March a Provisional Government took office. The Petrograd Soviet, which was backed by the vast majority of the workers and the garrison, continued to exist alongside this middle-class government. Already on 14 March the Soviet had issued its Order No. 1 aimed at reducing the power and authority of the officer corps by providing for the election of committees of soldiers in all units. Measures were taken by the committee to prevent the control of arms by officers; saluting off duty was abolished. The power of the Soviet in the capital and in the army deprived the Provisional Government of effective military support and this weakness was to prove fatal.

Mannerheim's experiences of the violence in Petrograd were sufficient to indicate to him that the revolution seemed more likely to lead to mob rule or a socialist dictatorship than to the attainment of the sort of liberal reforms for which he had so long hoped. Instead of parliamentary government evolving in Russia by peaceful means, a revolution had resulted in the establishment of a Provisional Government that was not responsible to parliament, and which possessed – at any rate in name – dictatorial powers. Revolutionary change was anathema to Mannerheim. He had hoped that Russia would become a constitutional monarchy, and the extinction of the monarchy was a severe shock to one who had continued loyally to serve the imperial family in spite of the harsh treatment meted out to Finland by the Russian government. He recognised that the disappearance of the monarchy weakened the whole structure of the state at a time when strong measures were needed to fight the war and overcome internal unrest. The demand of the Provisional Government for an assurance of loyalty from the army was hardly consistent with the way it had come to power. De Witt asserted that Mannerheim never took the oath it required, contriving to be absent at the time. The Provisional Government lacked legitimacy – a point Mannerheim quickly noticed – and authority.

He watched the progressive erosion of discipline, law and order with alarm and horror, feeling himself merely a powerless plaything in the midst of the troubled elements. He had hopes that it might be possible to act at once against the extremists, and while on the way back to his division in March 1917 called on General Sakharov, the commander of the Russian forces in Romania, to appeal to him to place himself at the head of a counter-revolutionary movement, but Sakharov thought such a move premature. Subsequent attempts to rouse his superiors to action were to meet with a similar frustrating lack of success: at first many senior officers accepted the revolution because the abdication of the Emperor was considered as evidence that he had approved of the need for radical constitutional change. Nor was it easy to take action. One evening, during a regimental dinner, de Witt observed Mannerheim receive a note and slip away. Much later Mannerheim told him that he had been to a secret meeting with Generals Wrangel and Krymov to discuss the possibility of marching on Petrograd to restore order in Russia. Having considered the situation they had abandoned the idea because all communications were in the hands of the revolutionaries. With neither railway nor telephone and telegraph they would have to move in darkness, and in the face of very menacing propaganda.

The disintegration of the army, the outcome of the fall in morale after so much unsuccessful fighting and the sudden collapse of the authority of the officer corps that accompanied the abdication of the Emperor, spread from the depots in the rear to the troops in the line. The armies on the Romanian front were the last to be affected, partly because they were on foreign soil, but primarily because of their remoteness from the centre of the revolution. Mannerheim found discipline still good in his division and it celebrated his fiftieth birthday in June with a parade and festival in traditional style.[37] In May he was promoted to Lieutenant-General. His division took over a sector near Suczava. In June he was given command of the VIth Cavalry Corps, composed of the 12th, 8th and 3rd Cavalry Divisions.[38] Soon, however, the situation deteriorated. Neither co-operation with the soldiers' committees nor opposition to them could check the collapse of discipline.

Mannerheim wrote to his sister Sophie at the end of May: 'The atmosphere in which one lives is nerve-racking and exhausting. To bear responsibility in the conditions that have now arisen is a comedy. . . . It is difficult in such a completely changed situation to know clearly what duty demands. That I will not continue to wear uniform a single day longer than I am compelled to is, however, clear.'[39] He returned to the same line of thought at the end of August. 'Altogether, I do not know what is right, to go or stay and bear responsibility with no means other than coaxing when it is a question of enforcing one's will.'[40]

De Witt described vividly the situation in Mannerheim's division and corps after the outbreak of the revolution:

'Difficulties and disobedience began with the proclamation of Order No. 1 by the Bolsheviks. Even in our division there was a very unpleasant affair and a squadron commander, having been treated offensively by the soldiers, left the service. From that moment Mannerheim became the corner-stone of all the officers. He upheld discipline and the honour of the officers with all his might. Soon we were sent to the front. Surrounded by infantry eaten away by propaganda our position was unsafe. Regiments had broken up. When a regiment was in the trenches it was most difficult to get it relieved. In the course of time a relief was obtained 2–3 weeks late.

'Each morning General Mannerheim set out (with me and two mounted orderlies) through bivouacs and villages full of slovenly infantrymen hostile to officers. A group of four horsemen. The General in front, looking at the soldiers with a steely gaze. A miracle – never any trouble. From force of habit the vagabonds became soldiers again and saluted. For a moment. Afterwards, from behind, we heard, "Oh, but we are free now, aren't we?".

'The festival of the squadron where there had been a sort of mutiny came round. (Each squadron had a patron saint whose day was celebrated.) The General set out as usual. We approached the trenches. The horses were left with the orderlies. I followed the General. And then – he went in the direction of that squadron. The trenches were in the woods on a mountain. It was quiet in the sector. Taking advantage of the quietness, the General told the soldiers to gather round him. He made them a speech. "Dragoons, this is the day of your festival. I congratulate you, but someone is missing, your squadron commander, who often led the rest of you in action with great bravery, and who was always like a father to you. Have you forgotten the gift she gave you for the festival day of your squadron? You have treated him disrespectfully and today, on this festival day, you should telegraph to him to ask to forgive you." That was the sense of his speech and extraordinary courage was required to make it at that period of the revolution. Best of all, he obtained the telegram. But at the beginning of the speech the atmosphere was very unsteady.'

When a new army commander was appointed, Mannerheim arranged a reception for his visit. De Witt recalled that, after speaking privately to the army commander, Mannerheim sent him a message telling him to hold the reception for the visitor as he would not be there. Just before the dinner Mannerheim told de Witt, with an expression of distaste on his face, that the new commander had betrayed the army and, out of self-interest, had thrown in his lot with the Bolsheviks. After dinner the commander, who had disgusted everybody by his remarks, wanted to visit the dragoon regiment and above all bring up the affair of the squadron commander. 'The dragoons' reply was harsh and gave him to understand that the atmosphere in the regiment was against the revolution. The dragoons had already seen and put down pillaging and other disorders. Mannerheim arrived for the army commander's departure, half-lying (because of an injury to his foot) in an open car. Their parting was very cold. Later on, deputies from the Army Soviet arrived. The General received them, but before he did so had all the chairs removed except his own. It was his last contact with the Russian army.'

The summer was fairly quiet and although enemy pressure on his corps increased after the failure of the Russian offensive in Galicia in July, they made only local gains. The July offensive, inspired by Kerensky, who had become Prime Minister and Minister of War in a more radical government formed in May, had been converted into a rout by a sharp enemy counter-attack. By the time General Kornilov, who became commander of the South-Western Front, had secured the restoration of the death penalty for desertion and mutiny and checked the flight of his men, the whole of Galicia and the Bukovina had been lost, and the fighting capacity of the Russian army had gone beyond repair. Mannerheim felt that the position of the officers, though still far from satisfactory, had improved slightly during the summer, and would have improved even more had not the Galician disaster led to the prohibition of offensive action. A war of position, to which the Russian army was then restricted, could only be demoralising.

Desertion of the peasant soldiers proceeded on a massive scale as they returned home to share in the seizure of the land. Harassing of landlords had begun in the spring of 1917 and became more violent by the autumn. Mannerheim must have lost his own estate of Aleksandrovka in Voronezh Government during this period. It lay in the group of provinces south and south-east of Moscow which were especially affected by the agrarian revolution because of the prevalence there of the leasehold system hated by the peasants. The Provisional Government had no loyal armed forces to stop the seizures of land and factories and its insistence on continuing the war alienated the soldiers even more. The Bolsheviks, who had unsuccessfully challenged the government in July, were soon to come to power through exploiting the popular demands for peace and land.

The nomination of General Kornilov as Commander-in-Chief on 31 July was an indication to the Right that order might yet be restored. By the end of August Kornilov, a strong anti-socialist, had begun to prepare a *coup d'état* against Kerensky, who had appointed him. But Kerensky was saved by the vigorous action of the Soviet and the Bolsheviks, who mobilised the workers in Petrograd, arrested Kornilov's supporters and disrupted his troop movements. On 14 September Kornilov was himself arrested. The widespread support he had received from the officer corps caused all officers to be suspected by their men as counter-revolutionaries. Mannerheim stated in his *Memoirs*: 'The news of General Kornilov's failure made me realize that there was no hope of order being restored. Among the many who had believed that Kornilov was the man who could still save Russia there was deep gloom.'[41] At the time he had not been impressed by Kornilov's actions. He felt the restoration of officers' disciplinary powers would have been more to the point than the reinstitution of the death penalty. The failure of the *coup* merely made the situation worse. 'To crown all misfortune, came Kornilov's revolt, the inevitable consequences of which will be to deprive the high command and officers altogether of the little authority they have succeeded in preserving.'[42] The prosecution of military operations had become impossible. On one occasion he had to resort to shelling a division to get it to move into the trenches. He felt it was no longer possible to accomplish anything as a soldier in Russia. He was even powerless to protect his officers from mutinous soldiers, 'the last bitter drops of my already overflowing cup'.[43]

The VIth Cavalry Corps spent the summer of 1917 partly in the line and partly far in the rear, the 12th Cavalry Division eventually being ordered to the Odessa region for internal security duties.[44] In spite of the loyalty he felt towards Russia, Mannerheim had been wondering for some months whether to leave the army.[45] In September a badly sprained ankle caused by a riding accident gave him the chance to leave his headquarters, where the problems and the responsibility were becoming daily harder to bear. He went to Odessa for treatment and wrote from there to his sister Sophie on 26 September that he intended to decide whether to go back to his corps or to pull out. It would be hard to begin something new but he was afraid that no alternative remained.[46] The matter was decided for him by a telegram from the Chief of Staff of the 8th Army dated 12/25 September. 'By telegram number 14841 of 9 [22] September the Commander-in-Chief has ordered that you be transferred to the reserve in the Odessa Military District on grounds of opposition to the present conditions. The cause of this is completely unknown. Nothing has been heard either from the army or the front.'[47] No reason was necessary: after the Kornilov revolt generals suspected of right-wing tendencies were being sacked as unreliable.

Mannerheim fully agreed that he had not satisfied the requirements of the time since the start of 'the army's democratisation, or rather destruction', six months previously. He had no intention of challenging the decision and was only waiting for the papers concerning his transfer to the reserve to come through before deciding what to do in the immediate future. He would, however, try to get to Finland soon, although the situation there was uninviting. He wrote to de Witt – then on leave in Moscow – that he had the choice of 're-establishing his good name' or

III.   The last years of peace. A picture taken in Poland.

IV. The First World War. Mannerheim with his men.

being retired. He commented that to re-establish his good name would
be to tarnish it, and he preferred to leave the service. His bitterness and
humiliation were great and he poured out his feelings to his sister Sophie.
'I would not have believed that after 30 years' service I would find it
repugnant to me to walk about in the uniform of the Guard Uhlans with
the Order of St. George on my chest; however, the last 6 months have
reached the point that you would rather forget you belong to the "Christ-
loving victorious Russian army" as it is called in the liturgy of the
church.'[48]

News from Petrograd was depressing but hardly surprising. The
Provisional Government, having survived the threat from the Right, was
now threatened by the Left. The Bolsheviks gained increasing support
from the militant Petrograd workers and in October began to prepare to
seize power. Kerensky did little to forestall the rising and on 7 November
the Bolsheviks won control in Petrograd. Kerensky failed to retake the
capital, and with the exception of Moscow, where there was fierce
fighting, the Soviet government was accepted passively throughout
Russia; there was no apparent challenge to its power. Mannerheim discussed with other officers the possibility of a rising against the Bolsheviks
but came up against the mood of apprehensive resignation and somnolent
apathy that had been prevalent in the country since September.

Mannerheim's stay at Odessa was prolonged unexpectedly by a strike
of tailors, which prevented him from obtaining any civilian clothes, and
he was unwilling to leave until he could dress as a civilian if he wished.
He stayed on in comfort at the excellent Hotel London – 'quietly situated,
with sea view' – until 3 December. By this time his ankle was almost
better, but he made it the excuse to obtain a travel permit to Petrograd.
He even got permission to take his military servant, Karpatyov, with
him, and eventually took him on to Finland. He had already said good-bye
to the staff of his corps, not without regret, and the Akhtyrskiy Hussars
gave a farewell dinner for him the night before he left Odessa. It was a
touching moment, a final tribute to a general they revered and idolised.[49]

He had managed to reserve a coach for his little party, which consisted
of two English Red Cross nurses, an English midshipman, three Romanian
doctors, Karpatyov, and Martin Franck, a Finnish volunteer in the
Akhtyrskiy Hussars who has left an account of the eventful journey.[50]
Hoping to arouse more respect as a soldier than as a civilian, Mannerheim
decided to travel in uniform. It was, to say the least, a risky time for a
general to be travelling. His coach proved defective and had to be

exchanged, and there was further trouble from soldiers who tried to crowd aboard, but eventually he got safely to Petrograd on 11 December. He stayed there a week, meeting many friends and trying in vain to persuade members of the imperial family to lead a revolt against the Bolsheviks. His friends thought the chances of a rising were hopeless and evidently did not subscribe to his own belief that it would be better to die sword in hand than to be shot in the back or have one's throat cut. He was deeply disappointed at their attitude, and although he remained convinced the Bolsheviks could be defeated, began to feel that perhaps it might be unwise for a rising to be led by a Romanov.

He decided to continue his journey to Finland, which had declared itself independent on 6 December. As a citizen of an independent state he felt justified in leaving the Russian army. Careful, as always, to observe the correct formalities, he obtained a certificate of his nationality from the Secretariat for Finland and took it to the General Staff, together with a letter stating that he had served in the Russian army as a Finnish subject and could no longer do so now that Finland had become independent.[51] All movement out of the capital was controlled by the Bolsheviks and the Secretariat for Finland was not permitted to issue passports. All he could obtain from them was the document saying that he was a Finnish subject on his way to Finland. His army pass from Odessa to Petrograd was his only proof of identity. The General Staff could not help him and he refused to approach the Bolshevik authorities who were installed in the Smolny Institute where his sister Anna had died. He went to the Finnish station and got on a train simply by showing his army pass, which the Ingrian soldiers at the check-point could not understand.

On 18 December he reached Helsinki, where his sister Sophie had been expecting his arrival ever since she had heard of his transfer to the reserve. His half-sister Marguerite and brother-in-law were away in Sweden and he moved temporarily into their flat, together with his servant. After spending Christmas with Sophie, he returned briefly to Petrograd, travelling on the same inappropriate army permit as before. He was drawn to the city by concern for the fate of his friends there and in particular by the desire to see once more Countess Betsy Shuvaloya. Nothing had been done to resist the revolution which he was beginning to see constituted a grave threat to Finland. He enquired of the Head of the French Military Mission whether Finland could obtain arms from the depots at Murmansk, but could not wait for a decision to come from Paris. He was soon back in Helsinki, and the guests at his sister's New Year's Eve party listened excitedly to his account of his recent journey north through Russia.[52] Mannerheim never went to Petrograd again.

On 9 January, 1918, his sister Sophie wrote about his return to their aunt Hanna Lovén in Stockholm. 'You can imagine it is lovely to have Gustaf here. . . . Naturally there is much at the moment that appears worrying to him, but he himself is in a splendid mood and at present, as far as one can tell, in excellent shape. To have life and health left after all he had to go through is already something to be thankful for, and for a man like him, with his ability and experience, there must be found something to do in a country where everything will now have to be built up from the ground. It is, however, strange to think how little one knows and how little the career one makes and the position one attains have now come to mean. The whole structure has been built on soft sand.'[53]

REFERENCES

1. Heinrichs, *Mannerheim Suomen kohtaloissa*, i, p. 104.
2. O. A. Ray, 'The imperial Russian army officer', *Political science quarterly*, 76, New York, 1961, p. 592.
3. Jägerskiöld, *Gustaf Mannerheim*, p. 287.
4. Cf. the discussion in Niiniluoto, *Suuri rooli*, pp. 90–4.
5. Heinrichs, *Mannerheim Suomen kohtaloissa*, ii, p. 41.
6. Jägerskiöld, *Gustaf Mannerheim*, p. 174.
7. *Prikaz*, 5/18 January, 1909.
8. *Prikaz*, 13/26 February, 1911.
9. Mannerheim, *Memoirs*, p. 77. Surveillance of officers and soldiers had long been a duty of the Gendarmerie. Cf. Jacob Walkin, *The Rise of Democracy in Pre-revolutionary Russia*, London, 1963, p. 52 and note 20, p. 259.
10. Yrjö Nurmio, *Suomen itsenäistyminen ja Saksa*, Porvoo, 1957, p. 252, quoting a telegram from the German General Government in Warsaw, received by the Foreign Ministry in Berlin on 1.viii.1918. 'Adventurous' may mean 'daring'.
11. *Prikaz*, 5/18 October 1912. On the Major-Generals à la suite see Mannerheim, *Memoirs*, p. 77, and the article 'Svita Ego Velichestva', *Entsiklopedicheskiy slovar*, XXIX, S.-Peterburg, 1900, pp. 157–8.
12. Niiniluoto, *Suuri rooli*, p. 33.
13. Mannerheim, *Memoirs*, p. 8.
14. Jägerskiöld, *Gustaf Mannerheim*, pp. 115–16. Mannerheim's allowance came from the Handkassa, the sum of money from the Finnish treasury placed at the direct disposal of the Emperor and used to supplement the pay of Finnish officers serving in the guards or studying at military academies. It was recognised that the means of these officers were often very modest. Mannerheim had already received support from the Handkassa when at the Nikolayevskoye Cavalry School.
15. According to Elias W. Pentti, he called on the Archbishop in Turku in 1918 to

ask his blessing on his work as Regent of Finland. *Vasasa*, No. 38, 11.ii.1951, p. 2. Nearness to death strengthened his respect for religious belief and he was convinced that 'higher powers' controlled the destiny of man. Jägerskiöld, *Gustaf Mannerheim*, pp. 271–2. He also had a practical attitude to religion, writing that in China, 'The teaching of God's law which exists in our educational establishments is replaced by ethics – which is definitely of more practical use'. Mannerheim, *Predvaritel'nyy otchet*, p. 159. De Witt commented that Mannerheim was unexpectedly superstitious. One day he had been greatly agitated to find only three candles on the table at supper. Three candles were said to foretell death because in Russia two candles were placed at the head of a dead body and one at the feet. When one of the regimental commanders, who had been present at supper, was killed the following day, Mannerheim was very upset, and remarked: 'There, the three candles.'

16. L. Mechelin, *A Précis of the Public Law of Finland*, London, 1889, pp. 54–6.

17. Edvard Hjelt, *Från händelserike år; upplevelser och minnen*, I, Helsingfors, 1920, p. 280. Adolf Törngren, *Från Finlands strid för rätt och frihet; personliga upplevelser åren 1901–1914*, Helsingfors, 1942, p. 314.

18. August Langhoff, *Sju år såsom Finlands representant inför tronen; minnen och anteckningar åren 1906–1913*, III, Helsingfors, 1923, p. 265.

19. Mannerheim's continued service in Russia and his political views were certainly discussed in the close circle of Helsinki society. Svinhufvud was initially prejudiced against him in 1918 because he had heard Mannerheim had done nothing for his brother when he was deported. Einar W. Juva, *P. E. Svinhufvud*, II, Porvoo, 1961, p. 102. Borenius mentioned 'a forlorn hope' that Mannerheim might have been appointed Minister-Secretary of State as he was 'personally *bien vu* by the Czar and might have had a chance of stemming the tide of destruction in Finland'. Borenius, *Field-Marshal Mannerheim*, pp. 62–3.

20. Mannerheim, *Memoirs*, p. 76'.

21. Quoted by Jägerskiöld, *Gustaf Mannerheim*, p. 121.

22. *Spisok generalam*, 1914.

23. Jägerskiöld, *Gustaf Mannerheim*, p. 122.

24. The account of the battle of Kraśnik is based on the following works: *La grande guerre; relation de l'État-major russe; concentration des armées, premières opérations en Prusse orientale, en Galicie et en Pologne (1er août – 24 novembre, 1914)*, Paris, 1926, pp. 73–4. Mannerheim, *Memoirs*, pp. 81–2. Ernst Linder, *Om kavalleriet; några krigserfarenheter*, Stockholm, 1930, pp. 35–8. Linder's description is based on Mannerheim's own official report of the action. Jägerskiöld, *Gustaf Mannerheim*, pp. 149–54. Jägerskiöld's account is based in the main on Jeletski's recollections.

25. The account of the battle of Opole is based on: *La grande guerre*, pp. 144–5, 166, 175, 179–80; Mannerheim, *Memoirs*, pp. 82–4; Linder, *Om kavalleriet*, pp. 39–48; Jägerskiöld, *Gustaf Mannerheim*, pp. 154–8.

26. Alfred Knox, *With the Russian Army, 1914–1917; being chiefly extracts from the Diary of a Military Attaché*, I, London, 1921, p. 100.

27. Paul Rodzyanko, *Tattered Banners; an Autobiography*, 2nd ed., London, 1939, pp. 157–8.

28. Jägerskiöld, *Gustaf Mannerheim*, pp. 268–9.

29. Jägerskiöld, *Gustaf Mannerheim*, p. 267.

30. The account of the battle of Opatów-Klimontów is based on: *La grande guerre*, pp. 340, 342, 352–5. Mannerheim, *Memoirs*, pp. 85–7. Linder, *Om kavalleriet*, pp. 51–5. Linder's description is founded on Mannerheim's recollections of the action.

31. Jägerskiöld, *Gustaf Mannerheim*, p. 169. The award was published as a supplement to an Imperial order of 17–18/30–31 December 1914. *Posluzhnoy spisok*. The citation was also published in *Russkiy invalid*, No. 29, Petrograd, 6/19 February, 1915, Ofitsial'nyy otdel, p. 5: 'HM the Emperor has most graciously consented to bestow for distinction in actions against the enemy the Orders 4th class, of St. George, the Great Martyr and Victor, upon [the following] Major-Generals, commanders of guards regiments: . . . The commander of the Independent Guards Cavalry Brigade, Baron Carl Mannerheim, of His Majesty's Suite, for having led the brigade with outstanding courage and skill in battles near Opatów, on 19, 20 and 21 September [2–4 October], 1914, when he covered successfully the left flank of the Guards Rifle Brigade, by holding out selflessly in heavy battles against superior forces of enemy infantry, which were attempting to capture Klimontów and thus cut off the rifles from the [river] crossing near Sandomierz. He repeatedly carried out attacks, recaptured Klimontów twice from enemy hands, and finally, on 21 September [4 October], having received the order to cover the retreat of the rifles to the right, towards Annopol, but having found out that they were retreating to the left, towards Sandomierz, on his own initiative, and disregarding the danger of being cut off by the outflanking movement of superior enemy forces, he held in our hands the sole line of retreat of the Guards Rifle Brigade.'

32. *Spisok generalam*, 1916.

33. A Russian cavalry division comprised 2 cavalry brigades, each of 2 regiments of 6 squadrons. In the 12th Cavalry Division the 1st Brigade consisted of the 12th Starodubovskiy Dragoons and the 12th Bielgorodskiy Uhlans; the 2nd Brigade of the 12th Akhtyrskiy Hussars and the 3rd Orenburg Cossacks. Divisions had 2 batteries of artillery; 12 guns in all. The total strength of a division was about 4,500 men and 4,800 horses; the fighting strength was about 3,500 men.

34. *Österreich-Ungarns letzter Krieg, 1914–1918*, hrsg. vom Bundesministerium für Heerwesen und vom Kriegsarchiv, Wien, 1930–38, ii, p. 244.

35. Jägerskiöld, *Gustaf Mannerheim*, p. 227, quoting a letter to Marie Lubomirska, 16.x.1915. On Haiworonka see Jägerskiöld, *Gustaf Mannerheim*, pp. 226–7. Linder, *Om kavalleriet*, pp. 55–8.

36. Mannerheim used the form Wrancza. The Group took its name from the Vrancei mountains in the Soveja district where it was fighting.

37. Martin Franck, 'En husars minnen av General Mannerheim från första världskriget', *Marskalken av Finland, friherre Gustaf Mannerheim; krigaren, statsmannen, människan*, Helsingfors, 1953, p. 91.

38. The corps command dated from 12/25 June, 1917. *Posluzhnoy spisok*. Mannerheim's seniority as Lieutenant-General was dated from 19 February/4 March, 1915; the date of the actual promotion was 25 April/8 May, 1917. *Russkiy invalid*, No. 139, 16/29 June, 1917, Ofitsial'nyy otdel, p. 3. The 12th Cavalry Division was evidently added to the VIth Cavalry Corps, formed early in December 1916 from the 8th and 3rd Cavalry Divisions. *Österreich-Ungarns letzter Krieg*, v, p. 599.

39. Jägerskiöld, *Gustaf Mannerheim*, p. 320.

40. Jägerskiöld, *Gustaf Mannerheim*, p. 324, quoting letter to Sophie Mannerheim.

41. Mannerheim, *Memoirs*, p. 118.

42. Jägerskiöld, *Gustaf Mannerheim*, pp. 237-8, quoting letter to Sophie Mannerheim, 26.ix.1917.

43. Mannerheim, *Memoirs*, p. 118.

44. Franck, 'En husars minnen', p. 91.

45. Donner, *Sotamarsalkka vapaaherra Mannerheim*, p. 106.

46. Jägerskiöld, *Gustaf Mannerheim*, p. 328.

47. Jägerskiöld, *Gustaf Mannerheim*, p. 329.

48. Jägerskiöld, *Gustaf Mannerheim*, pp. 239-30. Mannerheim was transferred to the reserve on 3 October, 1917. *Polsuzhnoy spisok*.

49. Franck, 'En husars minnen', p. 93.

50. Franck, 'En husars minnen', pp. 93-4.

51. Donner, *Sotamarsalkka vapaaherra Mannerheim*, p. 108.

52. Stig Jägerskiöld, *Gustaf Mannerheim, 1918*, Helsingfors, 1967, pp. 19-21. Berta Edelfelt, *Sophie Mannerheim; en levnadsteckning*, Helsingfors, 1932, pp. 208-9. Jägerskiöld corrects the account of Mannerheim's movements in Heinrichs, *Mannerheim Suomen kohtaloissa*, i, pp. 16-7. The use of the permit is mentioned by Donner, *Sotamarsalkka vapaaherra Mannerheim*, p. 111.

53. Edelfelt, *Sophie Mannerheim*, pp. 212-13.

CHAPTER V

THE YEARS OF PREPARATION

Mannerheim may possibly have expected to return to the country of his birth when he retired, but he came instead as a refugee. He had only the few personal belongings he brought with him from Odessa and knew nothing of the fate of his possessions in German-occupied Warsaw. The authorities in Helsinki were even unwilling to issue him with a ration card for bread since he was not registered as a resident there.[1] His career had been ruined by the revolution that was destroying completely the world in which he had served so long and so successfully. And yet his life was turned into a wholly new direction with scarcely a pause; on 16 January, 1918, he was appointed commander-in-chief of the Finnish government forces. It was a remarkable change of fortune, attributable, in part, to the discussion in previous months of his participation in their work by members of the Active and Military Committees concerned with the creation of a Finnish army. Most of the members of these committees, like Mannerheim, belonged to the relatively small number of families prominent in Finland, who were closely known to each other, had been educated together and had intermarried, and whose influence was to diminish only gradually with the establishment of the democratic republic after the Civil War. However, before his return to the country some people close to the government had considered him too Russian or russified to be suitable for command in Finland.[2] He had to prove his Finnishness. Mannerheim's successful adoption of such a totally different role as Finnish commander-in-chief represented a unique transformation and achievement, accomplished in the face of massive hostility towards him as a 'Russian' officer on the part of many Finns, particularly the *Jägers* and some Finnish-speaking peasants.[3] But in spite of his evident relief to have left revolutionary Russia and his absorption in the problems that confronted Finland, the experiences of his service in Russia could not be dismissed and forgotten.

He always looked back on his life in Russia with contentment. In his *Memoirs* he wrote: 'My thirty years of service in the Imperial Army were ended. It was with great expectations I had begun them in Russia, that vast and alien country, and when I now looked back on the many years I had worn the uniform of the Tsar, I had to admit with gratitude that my expectations had been fulfilled. I had entered into wider fields which had given me a broader vision than I could have had had I remained in Finland in the years around the turn of the century. I had been fortunate in belonging to, and in commanding, crack troops with good officers and excellent morale. It had given me great satisfaction to command troops such as these, both in peace and war. Also I had seen so much of great interest in two continents. But now the mighty country lay helpless and, to all appearances, in the throes of dissolution.'[4] He wrote, too, of 'the experiences in foreign lands that had prepared me for my task in the service of the Fatherland'.[5] The preparation was as unconscious as the choice of Mannerheim as commander-in-chief in 1918 was fortuitous. However, he not only acquired in Russia the military training and experience that were the reason for his immediate involvement in Finnish affairs, but the years he spent in Russia profoundly influenced his whole outlook and are of great importance for the development of his character and for shaping his policy as a Finnish statesman.

Mannerheim was a first-class regimental officer who became a very competent general. There was never any doubt in his mind of his capacity to undertake the responsibilities of command or high office. His strong will had rebelled against the discipline of the Corps of Cadets. However, severe discipline, which had seemed so pointless when enforced by unsoldierly teachers in a backwater of military education, appeared more meaningful set against a background of realistic and efficient training and a higher general standard of instruction in military subjects: he responded enthusiastically to the discipline of the Nikolayevskoye Cavalry School. Strength of will and self-discipline were positive features of his character that fitted him to command. He had a number of physical and intellectual characteristics that were of great value to a soldier. Rheumatism was the only defect in the strong constitution which he guarded carefully. He attached great importance to physical fitness and on campaign during the First World War rose at 05.30 to do gymnastics (Swedish drill) and take a shower contrived from a bucket and a rubber tube. He could sleep deeply and briefly whenever he wished. He could grasp a situation quickly and orientate himself on unfamiliar ground with speed and accuracy. He was unruffled in a crisis, though his quick temper vented itself over minor irritations, and disloyalty outraged him: early in the World War he was with difficulty dissuaded from hanging a Catholic priest in Poland who had refused to sell his men hay.[6] On the debit side of his nature must be placed a tendency to favouritism, both of units and individuals. He made no secret of his great liking for the 12th Cavalry Division when he became a corps commander. He favoured some people more than others, depending on whether they accorded with or offended his likes and dislikes. He never suffered fools gladly and could be bitingly sarcastic. Despite this, he was careful to treat all his officers fairly.

S. de Witt, who was sent to the headquarters of the 12th Cavalry Division in the spring of 1916 as commander of its reconnaissance detachment, experienced both Mannerheim's temper and his chivalry:

'While mounting his horse (he had two: the old "Panache" and a very fine young animal, "Chardache"), he gave me the order to set out for a cross-roads and wait there for orders. Morning mist. Somewhere before us was a river and, beyond, the enemy.

'A good hour of waiting. A Cossack came with the order of the Chief of Staff of the division – Rejoin headquarters at the village near the river. I carried out the order and reported at the house where I found the whole of headquarters assembled. General Mannerheim at their head. I made the customary short report of my arrival. At the same time the devil of a din (the explosion of several shells fired, and well aimed, in a salvo). Everyone jumped, the General included, and he began at once to shout out at me telling me off for not carrying out his orders (to be at the cross-roads). The Chief of Staff wanted to speak – useless! I had to take the road back again. In due course I received orders for a reconnaissance and in the afternoon I returned to headquarters. I found all the staff, with the addition of the four colonels of the regiments and the two of the batteries, on foot near a wood. As usual, Baron Mannerheim at the head of the gathering. He saw my arrival and waited to let me approach. Suddenly he took several steps towards me and said in a loud voice, "This morning I was wrong to tell you off. You had received an order from the Chief of Staff, he told me later, and you had carried it out, as you should have done. I was irritable and I wish to apologise."

'I believe it was the first time in history that a General à la suite of

His Majesty the Emperor (as he then was) had apologised in public to quite a young officer. That day I had lost three horses killed and my own mare had been wounded in the head, but I had gained a completely just and trustworthy commander. I was his man, and I not the only one.'

Mannerheim could judge character and capacity accurately – de Witt described him as 'a good psychologist'. He possessed the ability to handle men, to be able, by the strength of his self-confident character, to establish a moral ascendancy over them and thus to lead them, and also to know how to address them in terms they could understand. He could drive them hard and sacrifice them when necessary, but the losses of the World War curbed his recklessness and imbued him with a deep respect for human life. He learned the price of war and told the Finnish General Ignatius in 1918: 'I have ridden through Galicia and Poland and I have seen the ravages of war; one who has seen them does not bring such misery to his country on purpose.'[7] The Russian scorched earth policy disgusted him; so did the brutality of the Germans, though he respected a chivalrous enemy. Bravery aroused his immediate admiration and he had already proved his personal courage in Manchuria. Experience as a soldier had developed his predilection for order and method, his high moral sense of duty, and ideals of loyalty, service and chivalrous conduct.

His skill as a trainer of troops had become evident before the World War and the war itself enabled him to display his ability as a commander. At first, his eagerness to see for himself what was going on made him go further forward and become more involved in individual battles than was perhaps desirable for a brigade commander, who needed to preserve a broad view of the situation and over-all control of operations. He revealed considerable boldness as a tactician, particularly in the execution of deep turning movements behind the enemy rear. His flexibility of mind enabled him to take advantage of a situation as it developed and his decisions showed initiative and sound judgment. Although trained purely as a cavalryman and lacking the theoretical knowledge of a graduate of the General Staff Academy, he was able to co-ordinate the other arms with his own effectively and make good use of the infantry units that quite frequently came under his command. He did not always get on well with his chiefs of staff. Never bound by preconceived ideas, he was always prepared to listen to their advice before taking a decision. However, once he had made his decisions – which often conflicted with their advice – he would admit no further discussion but required them to attend only to the execution of his orders. He could be ironic towards staff officers, and even as Marshal of Finland sometimes drank the sarcastic toast of regimental officers of the imperial army, '*Za Zhomini*', to the memory of General Jomini, the founder of the Academy. But he did not neglect to apply himself when necessary to the details of military paper work. The Finnish artillery General Nenonen, who began his career in the Russian army, said he had never seen industriousness like Mannerheim's in a cavalryman.[8] The best evidence of Russian official satisfaction with his accomplishments was his advancement to the command first of a division and then of a corps. He left Russia with a high reputation as a commander and with great experience of modern warfare and of the problems involved in handling large formations. Comparatively few Finnish officers acquired such a reputation and reached such a rank.

Mannerheim returned to Finland having fought for Russia and the allied cause for over three years. In 1914, as in 1904, he sprang to the support of the Emperor and accepted without hesitation the rightness of the Russian position. He regarded Germany as an aggressor which had to be stopped, and considered war between Russia and the Central Powers as an inevitable trial of strength. His sympathy for France and England was strong and he was absolutely convinced – even after the revolution had reduced Russia to impotence – that Allied victory was certain. He was pleased that his family, being pro-Entente, like many constitutionalists, were on his side in this war, but some expressions of opinion in Finland about the war caused him concern. He believed the manifesto conferring greater freedom on Poland foreshadowed a different, more realistic and more liberal, approach to the other non-Russian nationalities in the Empire after the war. He felt Finland should show solidarity with Russia in its struggle for existence, and that the Finns, by their coldness, were missing a valuable opportunity to give proof of their good will towards a nation to which they were physically and constitutionally bound. His judgment of Russian opinion was sound. Even the Russian liberals, who were ready to admit that Finland had reason to be bitter towards Russia, did not understand the Finnish attitude to the war and what they heard of the service of Finnish students in the German army and Finnish hopes for a German victory.[9] The Russian authorities made no attempt to conscript the Finns but Mannerheim thought it would be a mistake not to organise a volunteer force to fight alongside the Russians. Very few Finns stood loyally by Russia during the war and those who did received scarcely any support.

Against the background of the fundamental division in Finnish politics created during the first period of russification from 1899 to 1905, Mannerheim must be considered more 'compliant' than 'constitutionalist'. Like the compliants, he recognised the considerations of prestige that made it difficult for Russia to yield once it had embarked on unconstitutional action, and was prepared for the Finns to take the initiative to re-establish contact between the sovereign and the nation, and for them to give ground if necessary to prevent the situation worsening. This was the line of the Old Finns, the party of Finnish-language nationalism, led by men who took a more pessimistic view of history and politics than their constitutionalist opponents, who believed in the ultimate triumph of justice, if only the Finns held uncompromisingly to their rights as embodied in the fundamental laws of the land. But the compliants would only yield so far, and in the autumn of 1909, after the commencement of the second period of russification, the Old Finns resigned from the government in opposition to illegal rule. Compliance had apparently failed because there was no Russian desire for conciliation.[10] The continuance of Russian oppression deprived the advocates of compliance of the foundation of their policy.[11]

Meanwhile, Mannerheim continued to serve the Emperor, whom he liked personally, but with whose policies he disagreed. He had earlier justified his continued service on the grounds that a soldier served a country not its government. Jägerskiöld described Mannerheim's political sympathies as 'liberal constitutional. But he also had a personal viewpoint on the question of relations with the Empire; he was better informed about Russian ideas than most Finns and therefore keen to avoid actions which unnecessarily sharpened antagonisms, but at the same time also sensitive to the slightest indication of political repercussions.'[12] In a Russian context, he was indeed a liberal, quick to perceive and criticise reactionary trends, and anxious for the creation of a government responsible to parliament. In addition, he favoured some measures of social reform both in Russia and Finland. However, he was less liberal-constitutionalist in a Finnish context. The tone of his letters suggests that he would probably have agreed with the Russian-born senators who asserted that the unicameral Finnish legislatures had become forums of 'extreme radicalism, insufficient prudence, and a deficient sense of responsibility'.[13] Apart from the class division in Finnish politics between the Social Democrats and the bourgeois parties, each of which included conservative and radical elements, the attitude of parties and individuals towards Russia was the most important dividing factor, greater than their attitude to the language question.[14] Jägerskiöld acknowledged the difference between the liberal, constitutional attitude to Russia and that of Mannerheim, but did not go on to draw the conclusion that it was precisely this anxiety to avoid a conflict with Russia that put him a good deal closer to the position of the compliants, a position which he retained even after compliance as a policy had apparently failed. 'Close personal friends of General Mannerheim' told a British diplomat in Petrograd in February 1918 that Mannerheim 'believes that good understanding with Russia is essential for Finland'.[15] This attitude was quite the opposite of 'the Finnish people', who were at that time waging a war against Russia 'such as it was, is and will be'.[16]

His views on Finno-Russian relations during the war conformed with his long-held conviction that the liberalisation of government in Russia could not be avoided indefinitely and that the ensuing political changes would include the ending of oppression in Finland and the restoration of harmony between the two countries. Ultimately, the March revolution did lead to the restoration of constitutional legality in Finland, but by that time the intensification of Russian oppression that followed the outbreak of the war had hardened anti-Russian feeling in the country. Finnish industry sent a Red Cross ambulance to the front in 1914 and it was gratefully received, but no volunteer movement developed to serve the Emperor-Grand Duke. There was, however, a clandestine movement to send young Finns to train in Germany, and from these men was organised the 27th Royal Prussian *Jäger* Battalion, which fought the Russians in the name of Finnish liberty. In his *Memoirs*, Mannerheim denied knowing of the existence of the *Jäger* battalion before his participation in the work of the Finnish Military Committee in January 1918.[17] However, it seems unlikely he could have failed to hear something of the *Jäger* movement – knowledge of which spread to Russia before long – and there is a tradition that he was told about it whilst in Helsinki in 1916. Since he wanted a Finnish volunteer force to fight in the Russian army, his attitude to the *Jägers* could hardly have been favourable.

Industrial circles, with which Mannerheim was connected, disapproved of the *Jäger* movement; they looked favourably on the Russian connection, which became very profitable to them during the war. They also feared that a German victory would be followed by German interference in Finnish trade. Pro-Allied Finns did not like the close co-operation with the German army which the movement entailed. There was sympathy for the western allies in various quarters – in some literary and scientific circles, in the shipping trade, and among people who had been influenced by residence in Great Britain or the United States – but allied sympathisers were relatively few in number. On the other hand, extensive cultural ties with Germany created favourable conditions for the development of pro-German sentiment. British and French pressure on Russia to change its policy in Finland had hitherto shown no visible results, and the protestations of the Entente powers about the right of small nations to self-determination did not, therefore, carry much conviction in Finland. The Finnish activists, who organised the *Jäger* movement, believed in armed resistance to russification and thought that a German victory over Russia was the surest way to put an end to the oppression and create the conditions in which Finland could become independent: support for their trust in German might increase, especially among the students.

The contrast between this outlook and Mannerheim's antipathy to Germany and belief in Allied victory was to cause many difficulties on his return. Members of the Active and Military Committees had put off trying to contact him in November 1917 because they were uncertain how he would feel about the close co-operation they envisaged with the Germans.[18] He was deeply opposed to German intervention in the Finnish Civil War of 1918, fearing involvement in the World War on what he regarded as the losing side, and believing – correctly – that the Germans would pay scant regard to Finnish interests. He expressed strong criticism of Finnish policy in a letter to his friend Hjalmar Linder in March 1918. 'That . . . German intervention was called for is the result principally of our countrymen's (responsible as well as irresponsible) obstinacy, lack of discipline and blind pro-Germanism, and of Svinhufvud's vacillation. . . . My impression is . . . that the Government at any rate in its present form, and its representatives abroad, are not equal to the situation and they will make Finland completely dependent on Germany.'[19] His caution in dealing with Germany in 1918, and again during the Second World War, was reinforced by his experiences in Romanias: what he had seen there of Russian disregard of Romanian susceptibilities had made him acutely aware of the care with which a small country should conduct its relations with a great power, and he was determined to use his authority to protect Finnish interests.[20] The naïveté with which Finnish politicians conducted international affairs horrified him.[21] Life in Russia, particularly in St. Petersburg, had helped him to acquire an

appreciation of great power politics and had enabled him to escape from the essentially provincial outlook that characterised the majority of Finns, whose vision was limited to their own country. Not only could he relate Finnish policies and events to the broader context of events in Europe, but he could regard them with a unique detachment. The Finnish activists were incapable of appraising in a detached way matters in which they had been so long and so intimately involved. Their approach to foreign affairs was thus far narrower than Mannerheim's although, like him, they possessed a knowledge of languages which helped them to make contacts abroad. Mannerheim's fluent French – the language spoken in his Russian home and in which he always wrote to his daughters – was to be an asset in the diplomatic negotiations he undertook in 1918 and 1919; his sound judgment of people was also invaluable in this connection.

Absence from Finland did not mean of itself that Mannerheim was alienated from the country or uninformed about it. Although his continued service in Russia was offensive from the constitutionalist standpoint, he had never condoned the russification policy, and retained a regard for legality and order. It had amazed and shocked him to read in November 1905 of the Governor-General of Finland holding discussions with revolutionaries. Revolution was not something to parley with. He looked to a strong executive to uphold the national interest, maintain stable government and the rule of law, and overcome what he regarded as the divisive and irresponsible influence of party politics, for which he had no sympathy. His loyalty lay to the country, not to any party. He believed political liberty should be linked to political responsibility and that universal suffrage and parliamentary democracy should not be conceded to a politically immature society. He accepted without question the obligations – and privileges – of rank, and although his attitude was based firmly on concepts of responsibility, justice, and honour, it left no room for democracy. Leo Mechelin, an old friend of Count Carl Robert Mannerheim, wrote that under the old constitution, 'the nobles have retained a precious privilege by way of legacy from past ages – that of constituting a part of the Diet. . . . But if this right of representation is a privilege, which is beyond all doubt, it implies at the same time a public duty, a political function outside the pale of the common law.'[22] Mannerheim had been brought up in this tradition and was reluctant for the nobility to surrender its constitutional privilege and its political duty to members of society inferior in education and experience of affairs. He thought the Finnish parliamentary reform of 1906 too far-reaching and that the events of 1918 proved that the people were not ready to take the responsibility such a reform entailed.[23] The March revolution was not at all the gradual liberalisation he had been hoping for in Russia. The removal of the stabilising influence of the monarchy, the very provisional nature of the new government and its reluctance and inability to suppress the subversive element of the extreme left, released violent political passions before which law and order broke down. This permitted the ruthlessly determined Bolsheviks to exploit the situation to seize power, terrorise and destroy the elements of society to which they were opposed, and establish a vicious dictatorship.[24]

Mannerheim was implacably opposed to Bolshevism, which he did not believe to be an ideal that was Russian by nature. 'Mannerheim was a soldier of tradition, who looked upon the revolution at bottom as an anarchistic and defeatist phenomenon. . . . Since Mannerheim was conservative in his outlook and a representative of an aristocratic way of life, Bolshevism in his eyes was tantamount to mob rule, the violent enemy of traditional values, with which no compromise could come into question.'[25] Bolshevism was a denial of legality and liberty and its aim was only a dream, incapable of fulfilment.[26] He perceived the menacing significance of the Russian revolution, not least for Finland, where he recognised on his return the same conditions of social chaos and political indecision that had resulted in Russia in a Bolshevist dictatorship. Kept in touch with Finland by occasional visits, correspondence with his relatives, contact with fellow-countrymen in Russia, and a fairly regular supply of the Swedish-language Helsinki newspaper *Hufvudstadsbladet*, he viewed with alarm the 'short-sighted' and 'brazen' demands of the socialist majority in the Finnish parliament in 1917.[27] He feared that the wave of terror from the east would sweep across Finland and was concerned, even before his return, to prevent it happening.[28]

The course of the Russian revolution had probably convinced him by the autumn of 1917 of the desirability of Finland severing its connection with Russia and becoming independent. However, he never lost sight of the situation in Russia and continued to recognise the extent to which the two countries were bound together by their geographical contiguity and Finland's strategic importance to the security of Petrograd. He hoped to create in Finland a base from which to launch an attack on Soviet-held Petrograd and establish there a counter-revolutionary government with which Finland could live in peace. This concept of the task of the Finnish White Army was his alone and, although a few conservatives of his generation supported him, he was unable to persuade Finnish leaders to agree to a policy of intervention, particularly since he was unable to obtain recognition of Finnish independence from the Russian Whites. He believed Finland's only hope of accomplishing its aim of acquiring Eastern Karelia without endangering good relations with a future Russian state lay in its taking part at the same time in the suppression of Bolshevism in Russia. Great mistrust was aroused in Finland by his inability to speak Finnish, a language he had not needed since passing the matriculation examination; his connections with Russia and evident sympathy for a country so hated by the generations that had grown up during the years of oppression, intensified suspicion of him. Nor were Finns able to differentiate, as he was, between White and Red Russians – all were equally to be condemned. Edvard Hjelt, one of the pro-German leaders of the *Jäger* movement, pointed out to Svinhufvud that Mannerheim did not wage war against Russia but against the Red gangs. There was a danger that industrialists, men of commerce, and older conservatives would be attracted by his views and form a party round him.[29]

Finnish politicians, including Hjelt, were naturally alienated also by evidence of Mannerheim's undemocratic views, and by his authoritarian reluctance to share with them the responsibility of office. Except in times of crisis, however, the politicians could afford to ignore Mannerheim because of his political isolation: he remained a leader without a party and his political influence in a democratic state was therefore limited. Mannerheim's antipathy to party politics precluded the possibility that he might attempt to enhance his political influence by organising into a mass party the large personal following he had acquired in the country as the victorious commander-in-chief of 1918.

The years of preparation in Russia thus constituted both advantages and disadvantages for Mannerheim when he returned to Finland. Service in Russia had endowed him with knowledge and experience that fitted him to serve his country, but had also accentuated the dissimilarities between an untypical Finn and his fellow-countrymen. Although he described Russia in his *Memoirs* as 'alien', he had felt anything but alien in the social milieu in which he had lived there. From the time when he stayed on his godmother's estate at Lukianovka in 1887, he felt completely at ease in the atmosphere of European culture in which the Russian aristocratic and high official and military classes lived. Little or no attention was paid to the nationality of those admitted to Russian society, and in his own social relationships throughout life Mannerheim showed a similar lack of prejudice. The style of life he observed in Russia – generally impressive and at times magnificent – appealed to him: he enjoyed living in a grand manner. These early experiences in Russia also stimulated his ambition and the urge to escape from Finland, which the circumstances of his adolescence had made seem a restricted and even petty environment. Had he not been expelled from the Corps of Cadets, he afterwards joked, he might have become postmaster at Heinola. He had left Finland to seek adventure and glory in the wider world of the Russian Empire. He had found both, and in return served the Emperor faithfully and loyally through difficult times. After the revolution such aims and ideals appeared increasingly anachronistic in a century of materialism. There was less regard for the virtues he acknowledged and pursued with relentless determination – honour, fame, courage, dignity. His remark that he could die in peace after receiving the Order of St. George, and his argument that it would be better to die sword in hand than to be murdered by the Bolsheviks, afford glimpses of his attitude to life. 'He was a cosmopolite in the age of nationalism; an aristocrat in the age of democracy; a conservative in the age of revolutions. These facts were at the same time his glory and his tragedy.'[30] This contrast between the man and his time became the essential problem of his life after his return to Finland.

Mannerheim's Russian background, cosmopolitan outlook, sense of honour, and ambition prompted his interventionist policy in 1918 and 1919 which his opponents have seen as evidence of a callous indifference to Finnish interests. 'This war aim involved the obvious danger of the destruction of the Finnish people's long held endeavour for the right of self-determination, which had at last been attained quite recently. That Mannerheim urged Finland to set out voluntarily on such a hazardous adventure indicates clearly that he did not possess a Finnish turn of mind and had no feeling of responsibility for the fate of the Finnish people.'[31] At the time, the revelation of the 'White General' as an interventionist shocked his Finnish supporters, who were unmoved by his arguments and did nothing to assist his policy. He was not, in fact, indifferent to Finnish interests as the terms of his agreement with Yudenich, his opposition to German intervention, and his determination to prevent Sweden from acquiring the Åland islands showed, but without doubt he experienced a conflict between his duty to the new Finland and a wider obligation, indeed a personal responsibility and point of honour, to crush

Bolshevism in the interests of Russia and of civilisation as a whole. He actually stated that he considered the struggle against Bolshevism to be his life's mission.[32] It was this concept of his task that led him to describe his victory at Tampere in April 1918 as significant not only for the freedom and independence of Finland but also as a victory of civilisation over the Russian Bolsheviks and their doctrines of world revolution and destruction.[33] Nor did he exaggerate when he wrote in his *Memoirs* that 'Europe and the whole world have had to pay a heavy price for allowing Bolshevism free play in 1919'.[34] Opposition to Bolshevism did not, however, blind him to Russia's enduring strategic interest in Finland, and he was prepared to make territorial concessions to the Soviet Union at the time of the abortive negotiations which preceded the outbreak of the Winter War in 1939. In that respect, too, he was influenced by his experience of Russia and understanding of Russian aims. Recognising Finland's weakness in relation to its eastern neighbour, he was not prepared to antagonise Russia. Although the present Finnish policy of conciliation towards the Soviet Union is associated with the name of J. K. Paasikivi, Mannerheim shared the responsibility for its inception during his presidency from 1944 to 1946.

It has been stated that, 'The land that the eventual Marshal of Finland loved most was not his homeland, but pre-revolutionary Russia. Only when the latter was forever dead did he attempt to learn the Finnish language and the language of Finnish politics. Neither attempt was completely successful.'[35] Mannerheim probably loved Russia as a land in which he could pursue his ambitions, develop his talents, and live contentedly, and although he felt it alien in some respects, he certainly identified himself with the Russian state in times of crisis, feeling joy at its victories and sadness at its defeats. Sir Esmé Howard reported from Stockholm in 1918 that Mannerheim was obviously deeply attached to the Russian people.[36] Above all, he had a great and lasting affection for the Russian monarchy. Inscribed photographs of the Emperor and of members of the imperial family occupied a prominent place in his home in Helsinki, to the surprise of some of his Finnish visitors. He called on the dowager Empress Maria Fyodorovna on several occasions in the 1920s when he was passing through Copenhagen and 'had the opportunity to offer my former Colonel-in-Chief my homage'.[37] As a monarchist who considered it advantageous to have a head of state brought up for the task from childhood,[38] he had a natural predilection for the Russian monarchy, even if he preferred constitutional monarchy on Finnish lines to the Russian autocracy. The Russian monarchy imposed on men like himself a willingly accepted obligation of service in return for exceptional opportunities and social advantages. Naturally, it was not easy to accept the removal of the Emperor, the spiritual and ideological centre on which his existence as a regular officer had rested, nor to accept the destruction of the political and social framework within which he had lived so long, so happily, and so successfully. However, force of circumstances compelled him to adjust himself to conform more to the nationalistic image created for him in 1918 as the liberator of Finland and, as the years passed, this role became increasingly acceptable, both to Mannerheim and to the Finns.[39] The 'White General' became a national figure who was anxiously consulted and called to lead Finland in periods of crisis, but the difference between his outlook and that of the majority of Finnish politicians precluded his acceptance by them in more peaceful conditions. It is the paradox of Mannerheim's position that he, a former Russian general, should attain a unique eminence in the history of his country as the Marshal of Finland.

REFERENCES

1. Edelfelt, *Sophie Mannerheim*, p. 209.

2. Donner, *Sotamarsalkka vapaaherra Mannerheim*, p. 104.

3. The British received first-hand evidence of the hostility shown to Mannerheim through the report of a British officer who passed through the Finnish lines in April 1918. Report to Sir Esmé Howard by Second-Lieutenant J. J. Hitching, 2 April 1918. F. O. 371/3209, 70384/57739/56. Opposition to 'Russian' officers is discussed, for example, by Aarne Sihvo, *Muistelmani*, I, Helsinki, 1954, pp. 356–7, 413–14.

4. Mannerheim, *Memoirs*, p. 124.

5. Mannerheim, *Memoirs*, p. ix.

6. Jägerskiöld, *Gustaf Mannerheim*, p. 263, quoting Jeletski.

7. Ignatius, *Gustaf Mannerheim*, p. 20.

8. Heinrichs, *Mannerheim Suomen kohtaloissa*, ii, p. 316.

9. K. G. Idman, *Maamme itsenäistymisen vuosilta; muistelmia*, Porvoo, 1953, pp. 92–3.

10. Eino Jutikkala, *A History of Finland*, London, 1962, pp. 233–4, 247.

11. Göran von Bonsdorff, *Suomen poliittiset puolueet*, Helsinki, 1957, p. 15.

12. Jägerskiöld, *Gustaf Mannerheim*, p. 133.

13. Jutikkala, *A History of Finland*, p. 245.

14. Jutikkala, *A History of Finland*, pp. 243–4.

15. F.O.371/3207, 30371/1827/56, 17 February, 1918.

16. Ulkoasiainministeriö. 1.P.k. *Min. E. Hjeltin poliittista raportointia v. 1918.* Hjelt to Svinhufvud, 25.iv.1918.

17. Mannerheim, *Memoirs*, p. 131.

18. *Suomen vapaussota vuonna 1918*, I, 2nd ed., Helsinki, 1922, pp. 370–2.
19. Mannerheim to Linder, 22.iii.1918. F.O.371/3208, 83059/1827/56.
20. Jägerskiöld, *Gustaf Mannerheim*, p. 254.
21. The letter to Linder, quoted above, shows that the adverse comments on the Svinhufvud government in his memoirs (pp. 185–6) were not merely retrospective criticism.
22. Mechelin, *A Précis of the Public Law of Finland*, p. 96.
23. Mannerheim, *Memoirs*, p. 24.
24. *Cf.* Mannerheim, *Memoirs*, pp. 127–9.
25. Paasivirta, *The Victors in World War I and Finland*, pp. 164–5. It was characteristic of Mannerheim's attitude to the revolution that, according to de Witt, he began to sign himself Baron Mannerheim only after the abolition of titles. He declared that the revolutionaries could not take away from him that which was inalienable, the title he had always possessed.
26. Jägerskiöld, *Gustaf Mannerheim*, p. 328.
27. Jägerskiöld, *Gustaf Mannerheim*, p. 289.
28. Martin Wetzer, 'Ett minne från ett sammanträffande i Karpaterna', *Marskalken av Finland, friherre Gustaf Mannerheim; krigaren, statsmannen, människan*, Helsingfors, 1953, p. 85.
29. Ulkoasiainministeriö. 1.P.k. Hjelt to Svinhufvud, 25.iv.1918.
30. Rintala, 'The politics of Gustaf Mannerheim,' p. 71.
31. Nopanen, *Carl Gustaf Emil Mannerheim*, p. 131. The American scholar Marvin Rintala has predicted that 'Finnish nationalists – for all practical purposes, all Finns – will in the future increasingly understand that for Mannerheim the Finnish nation was a means rather than an end, possessing at most instrumental value, not inherent value.' *Four Finns: Political Profiles*, p. 117.
32. Carl Enckell, 'Några minnen från mitt samarbete med Gustaf Mannerheim', *Marskalken av Finland, friherre Gustaf Mannerheim; krigaren, statsmannen, människan*. Helsingfors, 1953, p. 41. As British Minister in Stockholm, Sir Esmé Howard met Mannerheim several times in 1918, and saw him again in London later the same year. Howard wrote on 18 November, 1918, that he supposed Mannerheim 'would like to play the role of saviour not only to Finland, but also of Russia, for which country he undoubtedly has considerable sympathies, so long as it does not interfere with Finnish independence'. F.O. 371/3207, 191086/144/56.
33. 7 April, 1918. Published in *Ylipäällikön päiväkäsky* [Order of the Day of the Commander-in-Chief], No. 38, Mikkeli, 11.iv.1918.
34. Mannerheim, *Memoirs*, p. 236.
35. Rintala, 'Stig Jägerskiöld. Nuori Mannerheim', p. 301.
36. Jägerskiöld, *Gustaf Mannerheim, 1918*, p. 299.
37. Mannerheim, *Memoirs*, p. 9.
38. Mannerheim acknowledged that, in principle, he was a monarchist. Mannerheim, *Memoirs*, p. 222. *Cf.* Donner, *Sotamarsalkka vapaaherra Mannerheim*, p. 220. In 1918 the British quickly became aware of Mannerheim's strong monarchical views. Sir Esmé Howard, British Minister in Stockholm, reported on 29 July that Mannerheim disliked the idea of a permanent victory of the republicans in Finland although he feared the Finnish government's proposal to make a German prince king of Finland would commit

the country irretrievably to a [pro-] German policy. F.O. 371/3206, 132434/144/56. Mannerheim told Lord Robert Cecil on 15 November that it was unlikely that any other candidate would be elected if negotiations with Prince Friedrich Karl of Hesse were broken off. 'He was evidently himself a strong monarchist, and suggested that perhaps the matter might be left open till after the Peace Congress, without disadvantage'. F.O. 371/3207, 190067/144/56. Mannerheim held that 'if the Åland question ruled out a Swedish candidate, a Danish prince might have been chosen'. Borenius, *Field-Marshal Mannerheim*, p. 231. His choice was the cousin of King Christian X, Prince Aage, who later told K. G. Idman, the Finnish Minister in Copenhagen, that Mannerheim had approached him about the possibility of accepting the Finnish crown if offered it. Idman had not heard Prince Aage's name mentioned in this connection in Finland. Idman, *Maamme itsenäistymisen vuosilta*, p. 314.

39. On the change in Mannerheim's political outlook, see Paasivirta, *The Victors in World War I and Finland*, p. 165.

BIBLIOGRAPHY

UNPUBLISHED MATERIAL

FINLAND

Mannerheim Museum, Helsinki:
  Christian Swanljungs anmärkningar, tillägg och förklaringar till marskalk Mannerheims memoirer.
  Posluzhnoy spisok komandira 6 kavaleriyskago korpusa General-Leytenant Barona Mannergeym. Sostavlen Noyabrya 1917 goda.
Sota-arkisto (Military Archives), Helsinki:
  M.275. Finska Kadettkåren. *Kadetternas straff journal, 1880–1885.*
  M.276. Finska Kadettkåren. *Uppfostrings komiténs protokoll bok, 1871–1887.*
  M.279. Finska Kadettkåren. *Attestationshäften för kadetterna.*
Suomalaiso-Ugrilainen Seura (Finno-Ugrian Society), Helsinki:
  Diary of Mannerheim's Asian expedition.
Ulkoasiainministeriönarkisto (Archives of the Ministry of Foreign Affairs), Helsinki:
  1.P.k. *Min. E. Hjeltin poliittista raportointia v. 1918.*
Valtionarkisto (State Archives), Helsinki:
  Langhoffin kokoelma. XIV. No. 111. G. *Mannerheims rapport berörande hans resa till Kina.* (Kopia).

GREAT BRITAIN

India Office, London:
  Political and Secret Letters from India, 1906–07.
Public Record Office, London:
  Foreign Office, *Political*, F.O.371, 1918.

PUBLISHED MATERIAL

MANNERHEIM

Only a small proportion of the immense literature about Mannerheim is included here. For a systematic list of some of the more important works see: Screen, J. E. O., *A Select Bibliography of Marshal Mannerheim.* Helsinki: Otava, 1967.

Memoirs and general works

Mannerheim, G., *Minnen*. Helsingfors: Schildt, 1951–52. 2 vols.

Mannerheim, C. G. E., *The Memoirs of Marshal Mannerheim*. Tr. by Count Eric Lewenhaupt. London: Cassell, 1953.

Beranek, August, *Mannerheim*, Berlin: Luken und Luken, 1942.

Borenius, Tancred, *Field-Marshal Mannerheim*. London: Hutchinson, 1940.

Bourcet, C. de, *Le baron Mannerheim, maréchal de Finlande*. Paris: Sorlot, 1940.

C. G. Mannerheim. Toim. H. Kekoni ja H. J. Viherjuuri. Helsinki: Kivi, 1937.

C. G. Mannerheim, Suomen marsalkka. Toimituskunta V. A. M. Karikoski, H. Kekoni, A. E. Martola. Helsinki: Kivi, 1951.

Donner, Kai, 'Mannerheim, Karl Gustaf Emil', *Kansallinen elämäkerrasto*, IV, Porvoo: Söderström, 1932, pp. 11–20.

Donner, Kai, *Sotamarsalkka vapaaherra Mannerheim*, Porvoo: Söderström, 1934.

Douglas, Archibald, 'Mannerheim', *Svensk tidskrift*, 38, Uppsala, 1951, pp. 69–76.

Durchman, Osmo, 'Sotamarsalkka C. G. Mannerheim in esivanhempia', *C. G. Mannerheim*, Helsinki, 1937, pp. 48–72.

Edelfelt, Berta, *Sophie Mannerheim; en levnadsteckning*, Helsingfors: Schildt, 1932.

Ehrnrooth, Gustaf, 'Carl Gustaf Emil Mannerheim (1867–1951); minnestal.' *Marskalken av Finland, friherre Gustaf Mannerheim; krigaren, statsmannen, människan*, Helsingfors, 1953, pp. 9–30.

Enckell, Carl, 'Några minnen från mitt samarbete med Gustaf Mannerheim.' *Marskalken av Finland, friherre Gustaf Mannerheim; krigaren, statsmannen, människan,* Helsingfors, 1953, pp. 31–44.

Hannula, J. O., *Mannerheim; vapaussodan ylipäällikkö,* Helsinki: Sanatar, 1937; 5th ed., 1942.

Heinrichs, Erik, 'Mannerheim som överbefälhavare'. *Marskalken av Finland, friherre Gustaf Mannerheim; krigaren, statsmannen, människan,* Helsingfors, 1953, pp. 45–56.

Heinrichs, Erik, *Mannerheim Suomen kohtaloissa,* Helsinki: Otava, 1957–59. 2 vols.

Ignatius, Hannes, *Gustaf Mannerheim; luonnekuva, puheet, sähkösanomat vapaustaistelun ajoilta.* Helsinki: Otava, 1918.

Ignatius, Hannes, 'Kaarle Kustaa Eemil Mannerheim', *Oma maa:tietokirja Suomen kodeille,* III, Porvoo: Söderström, 1922, pp. 659–69.

Kaskimies, Einari, ed., *Puhtain asein. Sotamarsalkka Mannerheimin päiväkäskyjä vv. 1918–1942,* Helsinki: Otava, 1942.

Kivimies, Yrjö, comp., *Suomen marsalkka tuokiokuvina,* Helsinki: Karhu, 1951.

Klinge, Matti, *Mannerheim; kuvaelämäkerta.* Helsinki: Otava, 1968.

Kolehmainen, John I., 'The Memoirs of Marshal Mannerheim', *American historical review,* 60, New York, 1955, pp. 429–30.

Kósa, János, *Mannerheim tábornagy,* Budapest: Vietorisz kiadàs, 1940.

Koskelainen, Yrjö, *Mannerheim, Suomen vapauttaja ja valtionhoitaja. Mitä hän on sanonut ja mitä hänestä on sanottu.* Helsinki: Otava, 1919.

Lesch, Bruno, 'Mannerheimin suku', *C. G. Mannerheim.* Helsinki, 1937, pp. 16–43.

Linkomies, Edwin, 'C. G. Mannerheim', *Oma maa: tietokirja Suomen kodeille,* VI, Porvoo: Söderström, 1959, pp. 44–57.

Marskalken av Finland, friherre Gustaf Mannerheim; krigaren, statsmannen, människan. Helsingfors, Söderström, 1953 (Skrifter utgivna av Finlands adelsförbund, 9).

Marski läheltä ja kaukaa. Toimituskunta Ea Rahikainen, Tauno Majuri, Reino Juhonen. Helsinki: Kirjayhtymä, 1964.

Niiniluoto, Yrjö, *Suuri rooli; Suomen marsalkan, vapaaherra Carl Gustaf Emil Mannerheimin kirjallisen muotokuvan yritelmä,* Helsinki: Otava, 1962.

Rintala, Marvin, *Four Finns; political profiles.* (Mannerheim, Tanner, Ståhlberg, Paasikivi.) Berkeley: University of California Press, 1969.

Rintala, Marvin, 'The Politics of Gustaf Mannerheim', *Journal of Central European affairs,* 21, Boulder, 1961, pp. 67–83.

Rodzyanko, Paul, *Mannerheim: an Intimate Picture of a Great Soldier and Statesman*, recorded by Anita Leslie, London: Jarrolds, 1940.

Sotamarsalkka Mannerheim 75 vuotta kesäkuun 4 päivänä 1942. Juhlajulkaisu. Helsinki: Suomen kirja, 1942.

Talas, Onni, *Suomen itsenäistyminen ja Mannerheimin muistelmat.* Hämeenlinna: Karisto, 1953.

Tuompo, W. E., 'Sotilas ja sotapäällikkö', *C. G. Mannerheim*, Helsinki, 1937, pp. 91–139.

Voipio, Anni, *Suomen sotamarsalkka.* Porvoo: Söderström, 1942. 5th ed., *Suomen marsalkka: elämäkerta*, 1953.

Warner, Oliver, *Marshal Mannerheim and the Finns.* London: Weidenfeld and Nicolson, 1967.

Works relating to Special Periods
1867–1919

Backmansson, Hugo, 'Spridda hågkomster': *Marskalken av Finland, friherre Gustaf Mannerheim; krigaren, statsmannen, människan*, Helsingfors, 1953, pp. 77–85.

Dalström, Harold, 'I Helsingfors lyceum': *Marskalken av Finland, friherre Gustaf Mannerheim; krigaren, statsmannen, människan*, Helsingfors, 1953, pp. 71–6.

Franck, Martin, 'En husars minnen av General Mannerheim från första världskriget.' *Marskalken av Finland, friherre Gustaf Mannerheim; krigaren, statsmannen, människan*, Helsingfors, 1953, pp. 86–95.

Inkinen, Antti, 'Vaihe Mannerheimin nuoruusvuosilta.' *Uusi Suomi*, Helsinki, 21. vii. 1962.

Jägerskiöld, Stig, *Gustaf Mannerheim, 1906–1917*, Helsingfors: Schildt, 1965.

Jägerskiöld, Stig, *Gustaf Mannerheim, 1918*, Helsingfors: Schildt, 1967.

Jägerskiöld, Stig, *Den unge Mannerheim*, Helsingfors: Schildt, 1964.

Linder, Ernst, *Om kavalleriet; några krigserfarenheter*, Stockholm: Seelig, 1930.

Mannerheim Sparre, Eva, *Lapsuuden muistoja*, Helsinki: Otava, 1952.

Nopanen, Arvi, *Carl Gustaf Emil Mannerheim vuoteen 1919 saakka*, Lahti: Päijänne-kirja, 1963.

Rintala, Marvin, 'Stig Jägerskiöld. Gustaf Mannerheim, 1906–1917'. *Russian Review*, 25, New York, 1966, pp. 314–15.

Rintala, Marvin, 'Stig Jägerskiöld. Nuori Mannerheim', *Russian Review*, 24, New York, 1965, pp. 300–01.

Screen, J. E. O., 'Marshal Mannerheim: the years of preparation', *Slavonic and East European review*, 43, London, 1965, pp. 293–302.

Wallenius, Allan, '*Mannerheim den blodige' eller 'den vita djävulen'*, av Otto Grimlund (*pseud.*) Stockholm, 1919.

Wetzer, Martin, 'Ett minne från ett sammanträffande i Karpaterna'. *Marskalken av Finland, friherre Gustaf Mannerheim; krigaren, statsmannen, människan.* Helsingfors, 1953, pp. 83–5.

1920–1951

Lehmus, Esko, and Kaasalainen, Harri, ed., *Presidenttikaskut; kaskuja ja tarinoita tasavallan kahdeksasta päämiehestä.* [Tampere], Lehmus, 1961.

Lehmus, Kalle, *Tuntematon Mannerheim; katkelmia sodan ja politiikan poluilta.* Helsinki, Weilin ja Göös, 1967.

Nopanen, Arvi, *Mannerheim uusimmassa historiassa.* Lahti, Päijänne-kirja, 1968.

Asian expedition

Mannerheim, C. G., *Across Asia from West to East in 1906–1908.* Helsinki: Suomalais-ugrilainen seura, 1940. 2 vols. (Kansatieteellisiä julkaisuja, 8).

Mannerheim, C. G. E., *Predvaritel'nyy otchet o poyezdke, predprinyatoy po Vysochayshemu poveleniyu cherez Kitayskiy Turkestan i severnyya provintsii Kitaya v g. Pekin, v 1906–7 i 8 g.g.* S.-Peterburg: Izdanie glavnago upravleniya general'nago shtaba, 1909. (Sbornik geograficheskikh, topograficheskikh i statisticheskikh materialov po Azii, 81).

Mannerheim, C. G. E., 'A visit to the Sarö and Shera Yögurs', *Suomalais-ugrilaisen seuran aikakauskirja*, 27, ii, Helsinki, 1911.

Bulletin du Comité de l'Asie française, 5. Paris, 1905.

Garson, John George, and Read, Charles Hercules, ed., *Notes and queries on anthropology.* 2nd ed. London: Anthropological Institute, 1892.

Geographical Journal, 27, 35. London, 1906, 1910.

Hedin, Sven, 'C. G. Mannerheim; Resa genom Asien', *Ymer; tidskrift utgiven av Svenska sällskapet för antropologi och geografi*, 60, Stockholm, 1940, pp. 161–81.

Hedin, Sven, 'C. G. Mannerheims Reise durch Asien', *Petermanns geographische Mitteilungen*, 87, Gotha, 1941, pp. 24–5.

Hildén, Kaarlo, 'Suomen marsalkka Mannerheimin Aasia-teoksen valmistusvaiheita; muutamia muistelmia', *Suomalais-ugrilaisen seuran aikakauskirja*, 55, v, Helsinki, 1951, pp. 1–12.

Hildén, Kaarlo, 'Voyage du maréchal Mannerheim a travers l'Asie 1906–1908', *Le nord; revue internationale des pays du nord*, 4, Copenhague, 1941, pp. 241–59.

Petermanns Mitteilungen, 55. Gotha, 1909.

Reeves, Edward Ayearst, ed., *Hints to Travellers*. 9th ed. London: Royal Geographical Society, 1906. 2 vols.

FINLAND

Bonsdorff, Göran von, *Suomen poliitiset puolueet*, Helsinki: Tammi, 1957 (Hyvä tietää, 7).

Conférence Politique Russe, *Mémoire sur la question finlandaise*, Paris: Fournier, 1919.

Enckell, Carl, *Politiska minnen*, Stockholm: Geber, 1956. 2 vols.

Hannula, J. O., *Finland's War of Independence*, London: Faber and Faber, 1939.

Hannula, J. O., *Suomen vapaussodan historia*, Porvoo: Söderström, 1933.

Hjelt, Edvard, 'Finlands kamp för nationell frihet: historisk-politisk översikt', *Finlands frihetskrig skildrat av deltagare*. I, Helsingfors: Schildt, 1921, pp. 7–71.

Hjelt, Edvard, *Från händelserike år; upplevelser och minnen*. I. Helsingfors: Söderström, 1920.

Idman, K. G., *Maamme itsenäistymisen vuosilta; muistelmia*. Porvoo: Söderström, 1953.

Jutikkala, Eino, *A History of Finland*, London: Thames and Hudson, 1962.

Juva, Einar W., *P. E. Svinhufvud*, Porvoo: Söderström, 1957–61, 2 vols.

Korhonen, Arvi, *Barbarossa-suunnitelma ja Suomi; jatkosodan synty*, Porvoo: Söderström, 1961.

Langhoff, August, *Sju år såsom Finlands representant inför tronen; minnen och anteckningar åren 1906–1913*, III, Helsingfors: Söderström, 1923.

Lundin, C. Leonard, *Finland in the Second World War*, Bloomington, Indiana University Press, 1957 (Indiana University Publications, Slavic and East European Series, 6).

Mazour, Anatole G., *Finland Between East and West*, Princeton: Van Nostrand, 1956.

Mechelin, L., *A Précis of the Public Law of Finland*, tr. by C. J. Cooke, London: Chapman and Hall, 1889.

Mechelin, L., ed., *Finland in the Nineteenth Century*. Helsingfors: Tilgmann, 1894.

Myhrman, Anders Mattson, *The Swedish Nationality Movement in Finland*, Chicago: University of Chicago libraries, 1939.

Nordenswan, G. M., 'Pojkminnen från gamla kadettkåren', *Finsk tidskrift*, 147, Helsingfors, 1950, pp. 118–29.

Nurmio, Yrjö, *Suomen itsenäistyminen ja Saksa*, Porvoo: Söderström, 1957.

Paasikivi, J. K., *Paasikiven muistelmia sortovuosilta*, Porvoo: Söderström, 1957. 2 vols.

Paasivirta, Juhani, *Suomi vuonna 1918*. Porvoo: Söderström, 1957.

Paasivirta, Juhani, *The victors in World War I and Finland; Finlands relations with the British, French and United States governments in 1918–1919*, tr. by Paul Sjöblom, Helsinki: Finnish Historical Society, 1965. (Studia historica, 7.)

Protokoll förda hos Finlands Ridderskap och Adel vid Landtdagen år 1905–06, Helsingfors, 1906–07. 2 vols.

Puntila, L. A., *Suomen poliittinen historia, 1809–1955*, Helsinki: Otava, 1963.

Pylkkänen, Riitta and Westlin, Per-Olof, *Louhisaari-Villnäs*, Porvoo: Söderström, 1968.

Rintala, Marvin, *Three generations: the Extreme Right Wing in Finnish Politics*. Bloomington, Indiana University Press, 1962 (Indiana University Publications, Russian and East European Series, 22).

Schulman, Hugo, and Nordenstreng, Sigurd, ed., *Finska Kadettkårens elever och tjänstemän; biografiska anteckningar, 1812–1912*, Helsingfors: Lilius och Hertzberg, 1912.

Sihvo, Aarne, *Muistelmani*, Helsinki: Otava, 1954–56. 2 vols.

Suomen vapaussota. Toim. Kai Donner, Th. Svedlin, Heikki Nurmio, Jyväskylä: Gummerus, 1921–28. 8 vols.

Suomen vapaussota vuonna 1918. Julk. Vapaussodan historian komitea, Helsinki: Otava, 1920–25. 6 vols.

Teljo, Jussi, *Suomen valtioelämän murros, 1905–1908; perustuslaillinen senaatti, viimeiset säätyvaltiopäivät, ensimmäinen eduskunta*, Porvoo: Söderström, 1949.

Tommila, Päiviö, ed., *Venäläinen sortokausi Suomessa*, Porvoo: Söderström, 1960 (Historian aitta, 14).

Törngren, Adolf, *Från Finlands strid för rätt och frihet; personliga upplevelser åren 1901–1914*. Helsingfors: Svenska litteratursällskapet i Finland, 1942 (Skrifter utgivna av Svenska litteratursällskapet i Finland, 290).

Upton, A. F., *Finland in Crisis, 1940–1941: a Study in Small-power Politics*, London: Faber and Faber, 1964.

RUSSIA

Bujac, E., *L'Armée russe; son histoire, son organisation actuelle*, Paris: Charles-Lavauzelle, 1894.

Curtiss, J. S., *The Russian Army under Nicholas I, 1825–1855*, Durham, NC: Duke University Press, 1965.

Dawson, Lionel, *Sound of the Guns: being an Account of the Wars and Service of Admiral Sir Walter Cowan*. Oxford: Pen-in-hand, 1949.

Documents on British foreign policy, 1919–1939, ed. by E. L. Woodward and R. Butler, 1st series, III, 1919, London: HMSO, 1949.

Ego Imperatorskoye Velichestvo prikaz, 1889–1912.

Entsiklopedicheskiy slovar, S.-Peterburg: Brokgaus, Efron, 1890–1907. 43 vols.

La Grande guerre; relation de l'État major russe; concentration des armées, premèires opérations en Prusse orientale, en Galicie et en Pologne (*1er août-24 novembre 1914*), tr. du russe par Edouard Chapouilly, Paris: Charles-Lavauzelle, 1926.

Guerre russo-japonaise, 1904–1905: historique rédigé à l'État-major général de l'armée russe:

    IV. 2. *Raid d'Yingkeou*, Paris, 1912.

    V. 1. *Bataille de Moukden*, Paris, 1913.

Gurko, V. I., *Features and Figures of the Past: Government and Opinion in the Reign of Nicholas II*, Stanford: Stanford University Press, 1939 (Hoover War Library, Publication 14).

Ignat'yev, A. A., *A Subaltern in Old Russia*, London: Hutchinson, 1944.

Katkov, George, *Russia 1917: the February Revolution*, London: Longmans, 1967.

Knox, Alfred, *With the Russian Army, 1914–1917: being chiefly Extracts from the Diary of a Military Attaché*, London, 1921. 2 vols.

Mosolov, A. A., *At the Court of the Last Tsar*, London: Methuen, 1935.

Österreich-Ungarns letzter Krieg, 1914–1918, hrsg. vom Bundesministerium für Heerwesen und vom Kriegsarchiv, Wien: Verlag der Militärwissenchaftlichen Mitteilungen, 1930–38. 18 vols.

Prikaz po voyskam gvardii i Peterburgskago voyennago okruga, 1899–1904.

Ray, O. A., 'The Imperial Russian Army Officer', *Political Science Quarterly*, 76, New York, 1961, pp. 576–92.

Rodzyanko, Paul, *Tattered Banners: an Autobiography*, 2nd ed. London: Seeley Service, 1939.

Die russische Armee in Krieg und Frieden, Berlin: Mittler, 1890.

Russkiy invalid, Petrograd, 1915, 1917.

Shkot, *Istoricheskiy ocherk Nikolayevskago Kavaleriyskago Uchilishcha, byvshey Shkoly Gvardeyskikh Podpraporshchikov i Kavaleriyskikh Yunkerov. 1823–1898*, S.-Peterburg, 1898.

Spisok generalam, Petrograd, 1914, 1916.

Spisok polkovnikam, S.-Peterburg, 1907.

Walkin, Jacob, *The Rise of Democracy in Pre-revolutionary Russia*, London: Thames and Hudson, 1963.

SELECTED PUBLICATIONS 1969-1992

Mannerheim, C. G., *Brev från sju årtionden*. Sammanställda av Stig Jägerskiöld, Helsingfors: Söderström, 1984.

Mannerheim, C. G., *Päiväkirja Japanin sodasta 1904-1905 sekä rintamakirjeitä omaisille*, Helsinki: Otava, 1982.

C. G. *Mannerheims fotografier från Asien resan 1906-1908. Photographs by C. G. Mannerheim from his Journey across Asia 1906-1908.* Ed. by Peter Sandberg, Helsingfors: Schildt, 1990 (Travaux ethnographiques de la Société finno-ougrienne, 13 B).

Jägerskiöld, Stig, *Mannerheim, Marshal of Finland*, London: Hurst, 1986.

Jägerskiöld, Stig, *Riksföreståndaren. Gustaf Mannerheim 1919*, Helsingfors: Schildt, 1969.

Jägerskiöld, Stig, *Mannerheim mellan världskrigen*, Helsingfors: Schildt, 1972.

Jägerskiöld, Stig, *Fältmarskalken. Gustaf Mannerheim 1939-1941*, Helsingfors: Schildt, 1975.

Jägerskiöld, Stig, *Marskalken av Finland. Gustaf Mannerheim 1941-1944*, Helsingfors: Schildt, 1979.

Jägerskiöld, Stig, *Från krig till fred. Gustaf Mannerheim 1944-1951*, Helsingfors: Schildt, 1981.

Mannerheim - sotilas ja ihminen, Helsinki: Yliopistopaino, 1992.

Meri, Veijo, *C. G. Mannerheim, Suomen marsalkka*, Porvoo: WSOY, 1988.

Selén, Kari, *C. G. E. Mannerheim ja hänen puolustusneuvostonsa 1931-1939*, Helsinki: Otava, 1980.

Tervasmäki, Vilho, *Mannerheim - valtiomies ja sotapäällikkö talvi- ja jatkosotien käännekohdissa*, Helsinki: Kirjayhtymä, 1987.

Virkkunen, Sakari, *Mannerheim. Marsalkka ja presidentti*, Helsinki: Otava, 1989.

Virkkunen, Sakari, *Mannhereimin kääntöpuoli*, Helsinki: Otava, 1992.

INDEX

CGEM = Carl Gustaf Emil Mannerheim. The letters å, ä and ö appear after the other letters of the alphabet.

AAGE, *Prince*, of Denmark, 140
Abdals, tribe in Sinkiang, 82
Académie des Inscriptions et Belles Lettres, Paris, 58
Active Committee, Helsinki, 125, 132
Akhtyrskiy Hussar Regiment, 12th, 106, 119, 123
Aksu, Sinkiang, 58, 59, 67, 70, 76
Aleksandriyskiy Dragoon Regiment, 15th, 34
Aleksandriyskiy Hussar Regiment, 5th, 93
Aleksandrovka, estate in Voronezh Government, 37, 117
Alexander III, *Emperor*, of Russia, 98
Alexandra Fyodorovna, *Empress*, of Russia, 112
Aminoff, *Baron* Gösta (Johan Fredrik Gustaf), Lieutenant-General, 29
Aminoff, *Baroness* Louise (Lovisa Emilia Charlotta), *née* Cedercreutz, 29
Andijan, Western Turkestan, 67
Annopol, Poland, 101, 103, 123
Ansi, China, 59, 68
Antell Collections, Helsinki, 61-2
Appriken, estate in Courland, 37
Arapov, Nicolas Ustinovich, Lieutenant-General (1825-84) (father-in-law of CGEM), 36
Arapova, Anastasia Nikolayevna. *See* Mannerheim, *Baroness* Anastasia

Astrakhan, 67
Austro-Hungarian Army, 99, 101-7, 110

BARKUL, Sinkiang, 68, 77, 80
Bergenheim, *Baron* Edvard Ferdinand, 27
Berlin, 40
Bessarabia, 112
Bezobrazov, Vladimir Mikhailovich, General, 105
Bibikov, Sergey Mikhailovich, Captain, 102
Bielgorodskiy Uhlan Regiment, 12th, 106, 123
Bilderling, *Baron* Alexander Aleksandrovich von, Lieutenant-General, 29, 32
Bobrikov, Nikolai Ivanovich, General, 48
Bolsheviks, 113, 115-17, 119-20
Borenius, Carl Tancred, Professor, 4-5
Borodino, battle of, 98
Breslau, 40
Brusilov, Aleksey Alekseyevich, General, 41, 105, 110, 111
Bukovina, 102, 107, 110, 111, 112, 117

CARPATHIAN mountains, 99, 105
Castrén, Jonas, 90
Cecil, *Lord* Robert, 1st Viscount Cecil of Chelwood, 140
Cedercreutz, *Baroness* Alfhild Elise. *See* Scalon de Coligny, *Baroness* Alfhild Elise
Cedercreutz, *Baroness* Louise (Lovisa Emilia Charlotta). *See* Aminoff, *Baroness* Louise
Cercle de Chasse, Warsaw, 94
Charles XI, *King*, of Sweden, 18

151